Lead Don't Follow

The Human Guide to the Puppy Mind

by
Jennifer Broome

TREMENDOUS
LEADERSHIP
Leadership with a kick!

Tremendous Leadership
PO Box 267 • Boiling Springs, PA 17007
(717) 701 - 8159 • (800) 233 - 2665
www.TremendousLeadership.com

Disclaimer
This book is designed to provide information about the subject matter covered. The purpose of this book is to educate on the first year(s) of a puppy's life. The author and publisher shall have neither liability nor responsibility to any person or entity with respect to any loss or damage caused, or alleged to be caused, directly or indirectly by the information contained in this book.

Tremendous Leadership's titles may be purchased in bulk for business or promotional use or for special sales. Please contact Tremendous Leadership for more information.

Paperback 978-1-961202-15-3
Hardcover 978-1-961202-16-0
Ebook 978-1-961202-17-7

DESIGNED & PRINTED IN THE
UNITED STATES OF AMERICA

Front cover photo: Jennifer Broome with Betty the Lab
Back cover photo: Betty Cocker

TABLE OF CONTENTS

ACKNOWLEDGEMENTS

From the time I was a little girl, I loved dogs.

Thanks to our neighbors, the Lissenden Family, who brought me into their lives, enabled me to experience puppy whelping and gifted me my first puppy, a beautiful standard poodle. To the Brouwer Family, who let me borrow their trained Labrador Retrievers to go hunting. To my parents, John and Shirley Broome, and my brother, Chris Broome, who always supported me and my passion for dogs, ultimately turning it into my lifelong career. To my husband Jason, who has always supported and truly loved each new dog I have brought into our lives; there have been many! To my many supportive dog clients who adore me and keep me busy. To all those remarkable past and present employees at Quinebaug Kennels (QK) who have worked so hard to support the dog training, wellness, and care mission, enabling QK to be a leader in the industry for canine services. To my close friends (you know who you are) who have always had my back. To the many dog training mentors who took me under their wings, coached, and supported me.

Thank you to Paul Mavis, who pushed me to take this step and write a book! To Dr. Kyrena Parkinson, my friend, cheerleader, Chief Operating Officer, and someone who has gifted me with unbelievable platforms to learn and grow professionally and personally. To Dr. Tracey Jones, author and publisher, life coach, and leader extraordinaire who helped me step by step through writing my first book! And lastly, to all those dogs in my life who enabled me to touch, teach, and learn from them. They are my true heroes. I will forever be grateful to these dogs that shaped my soul: Ginger, Breezy, Sassy, Valley, Elsie, Peety, Doozy, and Treat.

I cannot wait to hug and hold them all again someday. What stories we will share!

DEDICATION

To Ginger, my very own first dog. Ginger was destined to be in my life. She was a standard poodle puppy born in a litter of eight to a neighbor and dear family friend. As a child, I was enamored with dogs. I became a treasured friend to Choco, the beautiful chocolate dam that later whelped the litter. I was there for the birthing and helping with the puppy care. The family nick-named my favorite little female pup "Jennifer" after me and graciously offered her to me.

A stickler for rules and responsibility, my Dad put his foot down and said "NO." My mom, brother (Chris), and I – all in love with this puppy – were devastated. The breeder sold the puppy, and emotionally, we put my Dad in the "dog house."

What are the odds that one puppy, our 'Jennifer,' was returned from the entire litter?! Not because she was sick, a bad puppy, or untrainable. She was returned because the new family's little daughter was terrified of this standard poodle puppy! Now that's puppy providence!

When we heard the news, Mom, Chris, and I marched with purpose to our neighbor and swept *our* puppy up! We didn't care what Dad would say; this was FATE!

One little girl's fright was another little girl's delight! Since we did not need two Jennifers in the home, we all agreed to name her Ginger, as her young puppy eyes were the golden color of the spice.

Welcome home, Ginger. She was our best friend. She taught me so much and introduced my world to dog care, grooming, training, and love. As a ten-year-old child, I took Ginger to AKC obedience classes. My eyes were opened to a whole new opportunity to learn about training, responsible ownership, and companionship. I would spend hours grooming and brushing her. I went on to train Ginger to jump fences, leap through hula hoops, and do incredible tricks.

We even went on to win ribbons at local pet shows. One of the best tricks we taught Ginger was to only eat out of your left hand. She turned her head away when you offered food with your right hand, but if you changed it to your left hand, she would gobble up the treat. Our best claim to fame was Ginger's desire to ride on the bow of my Boston Whaler as we cruised the Toms River with her ears blowing in the breeze!

She was my bowsprit, and folks pointed in awe at our beautiful partnership. My Dad was equally enamored with Ginger. She was his sailing companion, travel companion, and field companion. Dad became a "poodle man" and owned two others after Ginger. He may just have wept the most when Ginger passed at the glorious age of 15.

I am forever grateful for Ginger. She touched the hearts and souls of all who met her. She was the one who started it all!

INTRODUCTION
By Shirley Broome

It's almost unbelievable, but my daughter Jenny didn't have a dog until she turned 10. Her love for those wonderful four-legged creatures was evident early on, as she volunteered to walk our neighbors' dogs just for the joy it brought her. Looking back, I realize this was her way of forging a connection with her unforeseen future—dedicating herself to what she loves most: puppy and dog training, whether for obedience or tracking wildfowl. Even at a young age, she took on the responsibility of caring for our neighbors' family pets, going as far as taking some of them for a boat ride in our little backyard lagoon.

A turning point came when Gloria, a dear friend and neighbor, invited Jenny to her house when her standard poodle, Choco, was giving birth. Not only was she given the chance to witness the miracle of new life, but she was also promised a puppy of her own! Jenny's persistence paid off despite her dad's initial reservations about adding a family pet. After three months, Ginger found a loving home with us. Jenny took on the roles of walker and trainer and even entered Ginger into puppy obedience events.

Today, Jenny owns and operates a dog training and kennel facility, Quinebaug Kennels, in Canterbury, CT, with her husband, Jason. I couldn't be prouder of their success. Jenny's enthusiasm, passion, and eagerness when discussing training methods are contagious.

Did I mention she now has a 'pack' of dogs of her own? They are all family pets, trained and skilled in hunting.

Happy reading and rearing!

Shirley Broome

FOREWORD

By Katherine Regan

I first crossed paths with Jennifer as a 50-something Grand Prix show jumper. At 28 years old, she immediately struck me as an incredible individual. I learned that her passion for dogs ignited at an early age. When I met her, I saw her with six crates in the back of an enclosed pickup truck. As the years passed, I witnessed her journey from a one person operation training dogs out of her farmhouse and outbuildings, to her fully-fledged commercial dog transport truck, to shuttle vans, and two state-of-the-art facilities.

I spent two winters living with her in a cozy 600 sq. ft., three-bedroom apartment alongside seven dogs. One of those was a very needy deaf bulldog puppy that she was raising for the renowned Tommy Hilfiger family! During that time, she took me to various workshops. She even bred my first competitive field dog—a loyal hunting companion for my husband and me. I followed her wherever she recommended to absorb all I could about raising remarkable dogs.

At these workshops, Jennifer engaged with the best handlers in the business. She was a sponge, eagerly taking on any task to assist the pros, from helping their field setups to managing their sound systems. Her aim was unwavering: to learn and grow. Beginning in 2010, I watched her fully blossom, gaining respect from her heroes and contributing her expertise to the field of dog training.

Jennifer's perspective is unique, shaped by decades of observing, breeding, and training dogs. She grasps the significance of canine manners, unlike anyone else. Her pursuit of excellence is unparalleled, making her a sought-after source for advice, interviews, one-on-one puppy raising, and adult dog rearing. I know how incredible Jennifer is at raising puppies. She has raised two for us and continues to train our others.

She is so thorough, as she is with everything, but raising puppies is a gift. Being able to trust someone enough and reap the benefits is a thing of beauty!

I've gleaned more about life and dogs from Jennifer than anyone else. During those early years in the Florida apartment, I noticed her bedside table stacked with books on becoming a better entrepreneur. She's in a constant state of self-improvement, seamlessly extending to her approach to dogs. Her steadfast confidence and validated assurance elicit positive responses from the dogs she trains. Today, her state-of-the-art kennel is unrivaled in its operations, and her influence has grown significantly, having trained thousands of dogs.

Jennifer understands the unique qualities of each dog, from genetics to temperament and early care. She invests time in evaluating her animals and delivering tailored responses. The success of her personalized approach has led professionals to entrust their dogs to Jennifer for proper training. This book will guide you in becoming the leader your dog needs and foster habits that nurture a happy and obedient pup. Read and absorb every word she imparts. Her words stem from true expertise, ensuring you'll relish years of companionship and confident control with your best friend.

PREFACE

You undoubtedly purchased or were gifted this book because you want to live with a balanced, stable, and happy dog. The path to this goal is dog training. What is dog training? According to Wikipedia, dog training is the application of behavior analysis, which uses the environmental events of antecedents (a fancy name for behavioral triggers) and consequences to modify the dog's behavior, to assist in specific activities or undertake particular tasks, or to participate effectively in contemporary domestic life.

According to the American Kennel Club (AKC), a well-trained dog is the key to a good dog. When you train together, an unspoken language builds between you through words, hand signals, touch, whistles, and other methods.

Since we live with dogs, invite them into our homes, and expect them to perform in our daily lives, it is our RESPONSIBILITY to provide them with foundational teachings as a means of communication, rules, and structure. As devoted pack animals, dogs thrive living a balanced life of establishment and order, exercise, safety, security, and respectful relationships with humans. When a human can equally nourish a dog's MIND, BODY, and SOUL, you genuinely have a stable, happy, and balanced dog! Now, let's begin learning how to make that happen.

In this book, I'll take you from the first idea of a pup through the first year of life. We'll cover the ideal while keeping it real and introduce you to concepts such as Point of Contact and The.Quiet.Kue™, two of the most effective training programs to guarantee success.

Thank you for beginning this incredible journey with us!

SECTION ONE
SETTING THE STAGE FOR SUCCESS

Why: Motive is Key

So, you're thinking about getting a puppy? As with anything, the most important foundation is to answer the 'why.' Below are the most cited 'whys' for wanting to get a puppy. We'll unpack each of them. Although everyone's heart is in the right place, it's crucial to establish your motivation for acquiring a life-long partner and new member of the family.

Companionship: Most people acquire their first dog as a family pet for companionship. Dogs are amazing creatures, and they can provide us with unconditional love, devotion, and friendship. Seeking a dog for companionship is a beautiful reason to get a pup! To seek the right dog, understand that each breed was thoroughly and carefully bred over many generations to have a job.

The more intelligent, athletic, and genetically bred for a job, the more that dog needs to work, so be prepared. A pup's goal in life is typically not to wait at the door for you to come home from your stressful, busy life just to cuddle. A pup wants to run, play, learn, and feel fulfilled. Suppose you genuinely desire a faithful, loyal companion. In that case, it needs to be a mutually respected relationship, and you must fulfill your unique dog's needs.

Family protection: This 'why' is a challenging and often scary reason to get a dog. If you are pursuing a true guardian breed, understand you have a loaded weapon that can go off any-time, hopefully only when you pull the trigger. The more you elevate a dog's role as your protector, the more they have the reins to bite (even the unsuspecting mail carrier or beloved relative).

Protection dogs require high levels of training, socializa-tion, and understanding that they are ONLY needed if you fear for your life. Otherwise, you and your family are in charge. Protection dogs should only be owned by experienced dog people as these dogs are often very dominant by nature.

On the flip side, just owning a well-trained dog of any breed can be deterrent enough to ward off strangers, so the simple presence of a dog amongst your family, in your home, and on your property may be considered protection (even if the attack comes from licking to death).

Companion for another dog: This 'why' is not a great reason to get another dog. When clients use this as a reason, I often learn that the first dog's life is not truly fulfilled due to the lack of leadership, training, and exercise, so the 'hopes' that another dog will make the first dog happier can be a recipe for disaster.

Two dogs quickly become a pack, and they begin to lead you! So, unless your first dog is stable, well-trained, well-behaved, and could be a good mentor for a new pup, think again. What's worse than one untrained, wild dog? TWO untrained, wild ones!

My recipe for success when adding dogs to your pack is to plan them at least two years or more apart in age. This timing allows the first pup to grow, mature, and receive essential obedience training. Don't let the previous dog raise your new pup; that is your role. Spending quality one-on-one time with pups is most successful, so they learn to bond with you and follow your leadership.

Saving a rescue dog or adopting a shelter/rehomed dog: Rescuing a dog in need is a noble, caring, and loving mission. However, reflect on the above reasons for getting a dog. Rescue dogs have suffered from some form of neglect. They come with baggage, whether they were born into stress under a porch at an abandoned home lacking medical care, early socialization, safety, and security or were left uncared for or abused.

There is not only a challenging emotional element with rescue dogs; there are also physical and behavioral challenges that go with this decision, often based on human compassion. Making decisions based on empathy rather than the ability to provide for a rescue dog's needs adequately or understanding the consequences that come with a rescue dog can be dangerous. This situation can equally be stressful for you and the safety of your family members.

Please understand that I am ALL FOR rescuing dogs. However, rescues of unknown origin, breed, and temperament encompass their own challenges. It is most important to put responsibility, common sense, commitment, and dedication before empathy, rash decisions, and the inability to appropriately care for a rescue's needs.

Purpose-bred dog (show/field/working): These dogs may consistently live their best lives with their owners. People seek purpose-bred dogs for jobs (hunting, competing, adventure sports, dock diving, agility, obedience, herding, hiking, search and rescue, etc.). Owners often research the breed, the breeder, and the genetics as their goal is to find the smartest, healthiest, and most biddable dogs to train specifically for jobs.

These dogs enjoy the ability to perform at high levels and intensities and are committed to their genetics. On the flip side, it is all too common for people to seek sporting-purpose-bred dogs because they love 'the look' or have seen highly trained ones and want one for themselves solely as a family pet. This rationale can be a train wreck!

Most purpose-bred dogs look impressive and sexy while working because they are satiated with intense work, training, and exercise. So, unless you plan to fulfill the breed's genetic needs, consider a pure-bred dog with less intense training and exercise requirements.

A Surprise: Ugh, NO, super lousy idea! Unless previously and specifically planned, adopting a random pup and gifting it to someone is just a selfish act. For the pup's integrity and respect for humans, let people decide when THEY are ready mentally, physically, financially, and with stability in their lives to get a pup when the time is right. It needs to be a mutually symbiotic relationship where the human is willing and ready for a dog, and they choose the best option for their needs and abilities.

A Gift: This reasoning is similar to the previous thoughts. Purchasing a pup for a loved one can truly define the 'Money CAN buy love' concept, but ONLY if someone previously planned this puppy and the receiving human is all in favor.

As you will learn, proper reasons, seasons, and moments exist to get your first pup. Proper planning prevents poor potential problem pups!

When: Timing is Everything

A close runner-up to your 'why' is the 'when.' They say timing is everything, which is undoubtedly true when adding a new puppy to your family. Here's a list of excellent points to evaluate for the right timing.

Time of year: While we cannot always rely on Mother Nature to provide the puppy stork to deliver our pup in late spring or early summer, this can often be the BEST time to get a puppy. Why!? Picture this: darkness by 3 p.m., freezing temperatures, short days, and you standing outside in your pajamas and bare feet with a flashlight, pleading for your pup to pee when all he wants to do is chase snowflakes or worse yet, not step off the porch onto the frozen ground.

We all have more time in the spring and summer; the days are longer, and we can spend more time outside with the puppy. Summer puppies can enjoy learning to swim, navigate life more comfortably outdoors, embrace children off from school, and experience the season where we all seem a bit happier.

Stage in your life: If you do not own a home, there are challenges. Dog ownership involves providing a dog with a stable and secure life. For young people still living at home, asking for permission before bringing a dog home is essential rather than hoping for forgiveness.

All too often, it can be more expensive or impossible to find adequate housing if you have a dog. Refrain from assuming that your landlord will be accepting of you bringing one home. There can be expensive pet deposits and even a limit on the number of animals you can have as a tenant.

If you are a growing family, a baby soon to arrive is often not the best time to consider a puppy. If your work entails a total commitment to travel, this could present challenges for a pup's successful and fulfilled home life.

Lastly, can a new puppy enhance your retirement or impede your freedom to travel? These are all-important thoughts for the pup and your happiness, health, and wellness.

Your age and capability/activity level: There must be an element of common sense, respect for a dog's needs, and your safety and sanity. If you are blessed to reach your octogenarian years, perhaps that 80-pound German Shepherd you loved in your 40s isn't the wisest decision. Conversely, a pup isn't in the cards if you prefer a more sedentary life or your once marathon-capable knees fail you. There are always older dogs, too, that seek homes.

An unsettled world: The global health crisis that began in 2020 introduced the concept of pandemic puppies. Yes, unfortunately, this is a category. While a new furry bundle of joy may have entertained the masses during the pandemic of 2020, being stuck, bored, and lonely at home should not mean getting a puppy was a good idea. First-time dog owners needed even more opportunities to seek help from legitimate trainers in person.

Puppies were extremely sheltered from other dogs and people. They were overstimulated in their home environments and conditioned to always be with their owners, creating neediness and codependency. Puppy sales were through the roof, and veterinarians were inundated because too many people were breeding for the wrong reasons—to make money. Puppies arrived into a volatile, stressed, and upended world as humans navigated the challenges of the pandemic.

In 2021 and 2022, we saw many owners say, "I got a pandemic puppy." These impulsive decisions caused much need for rehoming, rehabilitation, or restructuring. All due to impulsive decisions. Remember, adopting a pup is a decision you must be committed to for the dog's entire life.

What: The Need of the Breed

You've decided to bring a puppy into your life for the right reason and at the right season, but how do you choose the purebred or mixed breed that suits your specific goals and lifestyle? Denying the genetic abilities of your selected breed or mix can be detrimental, so knowledge is essential! Do you want an alpha or overachiever to win ribbons, a happy-go-lucky, easygoing partner keen always to participate, or a lazy couch potato happy to do not much at all and just be loved?

While the internet can be a valuable resource for learning about dog breeds, it's important to note that many descriptions often sound appealing, with phrases like 'great pet,' 'loyal to their family,' 'good with kids,' and 'easy to train.' However, the best way to truly understand a specific dog breed is to meet them in person.

Knowledge of the breed can be easily accomplished by attending dog conformation shows, field events, performance competitions, or visiting breeders and shelters. While breeders and owners may passionately advocate for their particular breed, it doesn't necessarily mean the breed aligns with your goals and expectations.

One critical factor to consider is the breed's genetic history. You should ask yourself if you can meet the dog's specific needs. Your leadership abilities must match the breed's traits and behaviors and surpass them for successful companionship. Additionally, you must be prepared to handle the breed's size, temperament, and physical and mental requirements.

Imagine meeting a dozen dogs of each breed or similar breed mixes of various ages. This due diligence can help you determine which breeds suit your goals.

Why do you want this breed?

Don't base your decision solely on looks, attitude, or unique colors. Only a handful of genuine 'companion' dog breeds thrive on love and attention without demanding high maintenance in exercise and intensive training. Most other dogs are bred with specific purposes like chasing, guarding, hunting, herding, protecting, retrieving, or pulling. With these dogs, you'll spend your training time nurturing and controlling these innate traits, often redirecting them from their historical jobs to a job more suited to your lifestyle.

For instance, a terrier (an earth dweller who burrows animals from their lairs) may be better suited to finding toys that you hide rather than digging your yard up to find their voles. Here are some great questions to ask you and those raising your puppy. You'll want to be sure you can answer yes to all of these. Otherwise, you'll need to begin researching or select a different breed.

- Are you committed to meeting the breed's needs?
- Can you fulfill its exercise requirements and activity level?
- Are you prepared for coat maintenance, grooming, and upkeep?
- Can you provide adequate mental stimulation?
- Are you willing and able to address specific health needs?
- Can you ensure the overall well-being of the breed?

Two Puppies are Better than One! Or are They?

So you get to the breeder or shelter, and not one but a pack of puppies runs at you. You fall in love with one, and another family member falls in love with another! Or possibly two pups stare into your soul, and you cannot help yourself; you decide to get both. This love pup bombing happens ALL too often. What is the outcome here?

Bringing two littermates or pups of similar age home can be a painless initial choice because when you feel lazy, burnt out, or don't have the time, it is much easier to have them play together. They babysit and entertain each other! Yippy! They form their little inseparable bond. How cute!

But here is the all-too-common reality. Yes, the pups are BFFs. But one will most always be more dominant over the other. So, while one continues to get empowered, the other continues to get beat up. While these roles may change back and forth at times, ultimately, one pup shines brighter. One pup may be faster, smarter, or just more of a bully. So, from a socialization standpoint, one pup rules, and the other gets shadowed. They become so bonded that the other cries and pines for their buddy, even when you try to take one somewhere. So you take both or neither. Often, it is neither.

Let's face it: two puppies are truthfully TWICE the work and TWICE the cost. When owners continue this route, we get the classic "Littermate Syndrome." Simply defined, they bond more to each other, and behaviors may include difficulty bonding with humans and other animals, aggression, separation anxiety, and reduced independence in training.

These puppies learn to rely on each other, and one becomes more shy while the other becomes bolder. The shy puppy may NEVER reach its full potential, and the bold puppy may be nervous and uncertain when separated from the one they know how to bully. These pups often become codependent on each other and fail to bond with their human family as strongly as just one pup would. And sadly, as these pups mature, they often begin fighting. So the strong suggestion here is DON'T DO IT! Respect the puppy and get one at a time!

Two puppies are twice the work, twice the cost, and twice the stress. If you made this choice, you must crate them separately, walk and train separately, and effectively double your work to do it right. Do the simple math. One pup under five months requires about 3+ hours of your attention a day. Two puppies are nearly a full-time job!

I did go against my recommendations recently with a litter of pups I had. The day she was born into my hands, I instantly fell in love with one of the females. I already had her named Gunnel ('Battle Maiden' in German). This German Shorthaired pup was beautiful, and I was hoping she would be the next beauty queen in my line of GSPs. However, while the pack grew at three weeks of age, Gunnel did not seem to grow. She was very much a runt. But I was already enamored with this adorable girl with quite the personality.

Meanwhile, as I showed photos and videos to trainers, my show handler, and friends, the consensus was, "You are keeping that gorgeous, high-tailed, flashy white with liver ticked girl, RIGHT!?" While the entire litter was beautiful, Gunnel was certainly about ¾ the size of her siblings. But I was already bonded to her. I also decided to keep the flashy pup since she struck a pose everywhere she went. Her presence commanded attention, perfect traits for the show arena and the field. She was named Gertrude ('Spear of Strength' in German), also known as Gertie.

I had quite a job those first months of rearing those two. With my breeding program, I have big goals for the show and the field, and I was eager to provide each of them with the best puppy rearing I could. Fortunately, since I train dogs daily, they became part of my workday.

They came down to Florida with me at just nine weeks old for winter training. Here I spent time with them individually, always crating them separately. While they did get play time together, I was careful not to throw them together to keep each other company.

I spent their first seven months allowing their personalities to shine with individual attention. It can be challenging not to compare the two and expect similar responses to training. Each pup has its own unique personality. Even though they are now two years old, I still treat them as separate dogs, and I do not allow one to overshadow the other.

Both girls are well on their way to their AKC show championships, and each has wonderful qualities for my breeding program.

Although they look different and have
different personalities, they have the
potential to be dual champions in
the ring and in the field.

Given their strong genetics and desire to be
leaders and win ribbons, I will make sure not
to put them in a predicament where they will
challenge each other and potentially fight.
So, while I kept two pups here myself,
I have meticulously planned their
upbringing and allowed each pup
to shine bright in its own right.

Where: Consider the Source

So you know why you want a puppy: the timing looks excellent, and you're committed to meeting the needs of the breed you've selected, but where should you go to find your new puppy? Like the other considerations, take your time reading to find out about all the different options to be sure you pick the best one for your situation.

A Rescue Dog

First, let's discuss the pros of adopting a rescue pup. I wholeheartedly commend those fantastic humans who desire to save an animal's life and adopt from a shelter! There can be many beneficial outcomes when adopting a shelter or rescue dog. The most obvious is that the dog was homeless and personless and needed safety, stability, and security. There is also quite an element of self-satisfaction in knowing that you helped save or improve a dog's life!

There is some truth to the "Heinz 57" mixed breeds, as they may have fewer health issues than some of our over-bred 'purebred' dogs. Seeking this route can also be much more cost-effective, if not free, to acquire a dog needing a home. Lastly, adopting from a reputable shelter or rescue organization will often allow you to return the dog if it does not work out.

Now, let's cover the cons of a rescue adoption. The common denominator with rescue or shelter dogs is that they are of unknown origin. These pups may have been born into stress, disease, and neglect, and sometimes, they can never fully recover or normalize from an early unstable life. They may forever be skittish, emotionally damaged, reactive, fearful, or aggressive. Who knows what these poor pups endured?

Rescuing a pup of unknown genetics means unknown size, temperament, and health issues. What you thought was a golden retriever mix turns out to be a Border Collie/ German Shepherd/Great Pyrenees mix weighing 97 pounds. Genetically, all the adult dog wants to do is herd, guard, chase, and run. Sadly, this may not fit your living situation, lifestyle, or capability to fulfill that dog's life.

There are much better and more responsible ways to acquire your new pup than meeting a rescue transport vehicle on the side of the highway to adopt unquestioningly. However, suppose you are a capable and experienced owner who can provide the best outcome for this little beast of unknown genetics and character. In that case, you may just enjoy this as another fun adventure in your version of getting your new rescue pup. Beware of acquiring a pup sight unseen, and please don't put your family or yourself at risk if you are an inexperienced dog owner.

MEET THE PUPPY FIRST!

Shelters

The most thoughtful and intelligent way to help rescue a puppy is to MEET the pup first!

Sue Sternberg has incredible information available titled "Understanding Sociability" with Assess-A-Pet Temperament Tests. It can help you understand which rescue dogs to save and why. Her personal and professional life is devoted to helping dogs and people live happily together through temperament tests. Her tests are built around the dogs' sociability. The lower the sociability, the greater the risk of future aggression. You can learn more about Sue and her test/work at her website https://www.suesternberg.com/.

Consider the future by asking and answering these questions:

- Will this pup be 30 pounds or 90 pounds?
- How is the energy level?
- Is this pup safe for your family?
- Can you successfully interact with this pup immediately, and do you feel confident you can stop behaviors such as jumping, biting, or dominance?
- Conversely, what if the puppy is fearful, skittish, and freaked out, as is often the case?

- Do you have the experience to help guide and lead this puppy to a more fulfilled, confident, and stable life, or will your empathy and love further reward and exacerbate their fear into a downward spiral?

Spend some quality time interacting with this pup and include family members. Very confident and dominant pups need as much human leadership as those who are wide-eyed, insecure, and unstable with a tucked tail.

Both extremes in behavior take even more canine savvy and experience to help mold, shape, and train a pup with emotional baggage.

A Foster Home (often through a rescue organization)

Many rescue organizations do not have their own kennel or shelter complex, so they rely on the goodwill of dog lovers to help temporarily house the rescue dog until they are adopted by an appropriate family. This can be a wonderful alternative to shelter life, and these caring folks take these dogs into their homes and lives in the hopes that they can help to socialize, train and provide shelter and security until a permanent home is found. When experienced foster families take these dogs in, they can help to provide these dogs with stability and learn more about their temperament, exercise needs, and trainability. This can be a fantastic opportunity for the rescue dog with the goal to match the dog to a permanent owner.

Unfortunately, there can be downsides to foster homes. Some people have a bigger heart than they do the capability to truly provide individual attention, rules and structure to these dogs, so their home may just be an unruly pack of dogs. This run amok situation can make it even more challenging for rescue dogs to settle into homelife and stability, and they may even end up neglected or faced with unstable packs that hurt their chances for adoption rather than help. A foster situation is another great resource to be able to meet the dog to see if you are compatible and capable of handling the dog.

Backyard Breeder, Ad Online, or Pet Store

Again, let's start with the pros. Pups from this category can be the easiest to acquire. Pay the asking price, and you will likely have a new puppy. There are no background checks, application processes, or likelihood of rejection. These pups are typically reasonably inexpensive from the backyard breeder or online ad. Pet store pups can be much more costly as they are sold second-hand and live at the store until purchased.

You may also be helping to 'save' puppies locked in cages at the pet store or in the back of a pickup truck in a parking lot. This type of rescue from a bad situation can make us feel good.

However, here is the sad truth. Most pups from a pet store come from 'commercial' breeders and puppy mills. These breeders keep dozens, if not hundreds, of dogs in cages, often in ruthless, filthy, and inhumane environments. The dams are bred heat cycle after heat cycle and then often tossed away when they can no longer produce. So, each pup you buy from a pet store cage may support this practice.

These pups are born into stressful environments, lack early human socialization, and are bred for money, not for improving or maintaining the breed's health. As long as they look like a Golden Retriever, German Shepherd, or other purebred dog, some sucker will fall in love. Conscientious breeders will not just sell their litter en masse to a pet store! They want to meet the owners and ensure their pups are safe, well cared for, and loved.

Backyard "breeders" typically are not aware of health testing their dogs. They often think that they have a GREAT dog, so this dog should have puppies, and they usually ask around for another of the same breed (stud or dam) to produce puppies. Show me the owner of a purebred stud dog who conscientiously commits hundreds if not thousands of dollars on health tests and performance titles on their dog and agrees to breed to a backyard-bred dog with no health clearances.

While backyard breeders may have good intentions, they often know nothing about health tests, proper puppy whelping practices, dam and puppy health care and diet, or socialization of pups in the first critical eight weeks of their lives.

Acquiring a pup from any of the above resources could ultimately lead to heartbreak and costly vet bills if your puppy has health issues that somebody could have easily prevented with health testing. So that backyard-bred $400 puppy may cost you upwards of $5,000 later for hip replacements or disease management.

Rehoming Situation

So you heard that a friend of a friend has this dog they can no longer keep. Yes, this is often another way people can acquire a pup. YOU could finally be this pup's savior! But do realize this pup most likely got neglected in its early stages through improper rearing, socialization, and care. The pup may have been too much for the previous owner, causing destruction and chaos (as all puppies can!). So bear down; you may have your hands full. Take the time to reflect upon the previous resources and information.

Just WHERE did this pup come from? Why is it getting rehomed? Are you willing and capable of re-training this possibly unruly pup? Rehoming can be a great option, but realize that these pups often come with baggage and unknowns.

To summarize, while the previous methods of acquiring a pup may be some of the easiest and most cost-effective upfront, each choice has pros and cons. And many people have successfully acquired puppies each way. They may have lived extremely long, happy, and healthy lives! Those are incredible success stories. Just understand the downsides and potential issues that can also occur when purchasing or adopting a pup from those resources.

Designer Dog 'Breeder'

What is a designer dog? A designer dog is an intentionally bred mix, typically of two or three true-breed dogs. It all started back in 1989 with The World's First Labradoodle, and ironically, the creator now says that his designer 'breed' creation is his life's regret. He even describes them as 'crazy' and a 'Frankenstein's monster' with significant health issues. He said that he 'opened Pandora's Box.' Designer fad dogs today have gotten out of control. They are most often created to be different or to get attention. Who thinks it is intelligent to mix a poodle and a Doberman, a Bulldog and a Shih Tzu, or a Saint Bernard with a Standard Poodle?

In the last 15 years, Doodles have been the most popular designer dogs we have encountered for boarding and training. These Poodle mixes mainly include Labradoodles (Labrador Retriever x), Goldendoodles (Golden Retriever x), Bernadoodles (Bernese Mountain Dogs x), Newfiedoodles (Newfoundland x), Whoodles (Wheaten Terrier x), Schnoodle (Schnauzer x), Cavapoos (Cavalier King Charles x), Aussiedoodles (Australian Shepherd x), Cockapoos (Cocker Spaniel x), and Sheepadoodles (Old English Sheepdog x). I find many of them cute as pups, silly, goofy, intelligent and athletic! Let's face it: people LOVE their Doodles! My first dog was a well-bred Standard Poodle. Poodles are impressive dogs, typically ranking in the top two or three as the most intelligent breed.

I often would joke when I first started to see Doodles in the masses at my training facility; I would think, "Oh, how funny, the intelligence and athleticism of a poodle with the work ethic and drive of a lab. You have a speedy, intelligent dog who runs away from you, plays keep away, barks a lot, and is crazy."

Due to the massive popularity of Doodles and the fact that I joke, "Doodles keep the lights on at our kennel," I am not trashing all Doodles. Some breeders out there strive to produce healthy dogs, and they perform various health tests on their dogs. They may begin with a well-bred purebred Golden Retriever and Poodle. They breed through several generations, creating first generation (F1's) 50% retriever with 50% poodle, and this first mating can vary significantly, inheriting different traits from both breeds. They will always inherit the shedding gene. The (F), or Filial Hybrid, means the pup came from two purebred dogs. F1 is the first generation, and F2 is the second.

When you get into backcrosses, you will see the letter (B) on their label, which means that the Goldendoodle was bred back to a purebred poodle (some bred back to the Retriever but not as common). So, as you read into this Doodle explanation, you will find terminology such as F1b, F2b, F3s, and more. Many Doodle breeders strive to breed hypoallergenic and non-shedding for allergy sufferers.

However, there is no such thing as a 100% hypoallergenic dog. Still, it is possible to find dogs that shed less and are better suited for allergy sufferers. According to David Stukus, MD, "Dog dander is what causes symptoms of allergy. It's not the length, style, type, or shedding of fur. Dander comes from saliva, skin cells, and urine. Unless your dog has no mouth, no skin, or doesn't pee, it will release dander into the air (https://www.nationwidechildrens. org/family-resources-education/700children/2020/11/ mythhypoallergenic-dog)."

Doodles were just the start of the designer breed craze. Now, it is popular to intermix purebred dogs just for something different. These include Cavachons, Siberian Retrievers, Weimadors, Shorkies, Chiweenies, Pomskys, Puggles, Morkies, and so on! You could imagine a board game, Name That Dog Mix.

Thoughtful and devoted breeders want to preserve the purebred heritage and strive to improve their dogs' ongoing lines through a breeding program. The last thing that they want to do is intermix their purebred dog. At the same time, I see some proof that there are designer breeders who responsibly health-test their purebred dogs before mixing; the unfortunate reality is that most designer breeders pump out puppies for profit over health tests and temperament tests. These dogs are being bred primarily as companion fads, not for actual purpose-bred dogs.

Due to their popularity, we see many designer dogs that are consistently plagued with severe health, structural, and temperament issues. The larger mixes often pace in their gait and have bad hips. They may have extreme coat maintenance needs that owners do not address and groomers cringe at. Groomers encounter these dogs with severely matted, unkempt coats, which is simply cruel and unfair to the dogs.

Coat types and colors are also a fad! Each purebred dog breed has accepted colors according to their breed standard. French Bulldogs do not come in blue merle. Labradors do not come in silver. White German Shepherds are not considered purebred. The 'rarer' the coat color, the more often that pup was bred ONLY for dilute or recessive coat colors and patterns. Those funky colors usually come with a myriad of skin, allergy, and health issues.

The sad truth is that designer breeders often breed subpar dogs lacking health clearances simply for financial gain. Lastly, consider the costs for these designer dogs. Due to their popularity, people are paying two, three, and even four times as much as an actual purebred dog.

Experienced Breeder of PUREBRED Dogs

According to the American Kennel Club, reputable Purebred Dog Breeders should have ONE goal in mind. That goal is to produce healthy, physically and behaviorally stable dogs that meet the breed standard!

A responsible breeder is determined, thoughtful, and diligent to breed for consistency, temperament, and health. Why on earth would they ever mix with another breed? As an established and experienced breeder, I know first-hand that not all 'breeders' are equal. Some attributes of a thoughtful and conscientious breeder involve a careful selection and vetting process to constantly improve their breed genetics and maintain a high quality for health, temperament, and commitment to the breed standard. Some breeders may only offer one litter yearly or less, while others keep several brood dams and breed regularly. What are some things to look for when identifying a proven breeder who truly cares about the health, wellness, and integrity of their pups?

A proven breeder is not only highly concerned about where their pups are going, but they back their dogs with a health guarantee and take them back for any reason. The breeder stays educated and informed on the best breeding practices and carefully identifies the known diseases within their breed. These breeders are often involved with their AKC Breed Parent Club, belong to regional or local clubs, and support the breed often by abiding by a code of ethics where like-minded individuals share similar values and goals, all in the pursuit of maintaining their breed standard.

CHIC: The OFA (Orthopedic Foundation for Animals) created the CHIC Canine Health Information Center by partnering with specific parent breed clubs to research and maintain information on the health issues prevalent in particular breeds. So, the CHIC has assisted in establishing a recommended protocol for breed-specific health screenings.

Dogs tested by that protocol are recognized with a CHIC number and certification. With the prevalence of over breeding dogs or subpar breeding programs, truly conscientious breeders can stay informed on the most updated research into canine disease and have a resource to test their breeding dogs. The CHIC program provides accurate information about a breeder's health testing results for puppy buyers. The goal is to reduce the inherited diseases within our purebred dogs so that our beloved dogs can ultimately live longer, healthier lives.

Be prepared! Breeders often like to meet you and intensely interview you. It is best to meet the litter's dam, other dogs in their breeding program, and/or sire (not always possible). "The apple doesn't fall far from the tree," so understand your pup should be a 'mini me' of the dogs you get to meet.

Quality breeders provide necessary veterinary health care for their dams and carefully monitor them throughout the pregnancy with proper exercise, support, and nutrition. They will often confirm a pregnancy after the breeding through a veterinary ultrasound. Then, the week before whelping, have the dam x-rayed to confirm the number of puppies. This practice helps breeders through the whelping process for the dam's safety and to know how many puppies are expected.

Puppies whelped by an experienced breeder are born into the safety of a whelping area with human contact. They are handled, socialized, and desensitized from the start. Puppies receive important early nutrition, vet care, and deworming.

A breeder will strategically assist in matching each pup's temperament to the owner. Let them help with this! While it is easy to choose the first pup that crawls onto your lap, that could also be the pup who may be the boldest in the litter.

The breeder can share the consistent behaviors of each puppy as they often have them marked and identified from birth.

Your breeder can be your first resource for advice regarding your pup's health, nutrition, and wellness. They are often more than happy to help. They can best guide you about specific traits and characteristics with their pup's development. Your breeder is typically your best mentor throughout your dog's life!

While we hope you will be thoroughly enamored with your new pup, a GREAT breeder will take their offspring back at any age, no matter the reason. Lastly, when it is time for another pup, you can often return to the same breeder and get another pup with similar traits to your previous one.

There are many upsides to purchasing a puppy from an experienced breeder. However, there are also challenges and disappointments. These pups may be tough to acquire due to waitlists and interview processes. YES, a GREAT breeder will interview YOU just as much as you interview them. You are about to embark on a journey with their genetics, and the more protective they are of their pups, the more they care about success for all involved.

These pups may be expensive; however, due diligence upfront hopefully means a healthier dog in the long run. You may not like the idea that the breeder may choose your puppy, but remember and respect that they have known these pups for nearly eight weeks, and matching the pup to the prospective owner is essential.

The breeder may even deny you a puppy. OUCH! Take it personally or not, but if a breeder does not think that you will be a good match, you may reconsider your breed choice.

That breeder felt their pup would need to be a better candidate to meet their genetic requirements and expectations.

Not all Labrador Retrievers are Created Equal

Within each pure-breed dog, genetic components based on the breeding program can veer off the breed's original AKC standard. The history of the Labrador Retriever breed goes back hundreds of years to their birthplace in Newfoundland, where they worked and lived alongside their owners. The dog is described as strongly built, medium-sized, and with a sound, athletic, well-balanced conformation that enabled him to function as a retrieving gun dog, with substance and soundness to hunt waterfowl or upland game for long hours under challenging conditions.

They also embodied the character and quality to win in the show ring and possess the sound, desired temperament to be an excellent family companion. Today, there are multiple 'variations' of the Labrador Retriever. The breeding programs in Ireland and England tend to breed smaller-framed labs with a more sensitive attitude. These dogs maintain a very athletic build as they hunt long hours in the field. In the United States, the Labrador has been greatly overbred, and sadly, there is quite a division and a considerable stray from the dog originally bred and defined in the breed history. The Labrador you see in today's AKC conformation show ring is massive in bone structure, heavy coat, overall substance, and outrageous weight. It is almost expected (due to judging practices and politics) that the once athletic, purpose-bred dog is now egregiously 10 to 20 pounds overweight in the show ring!

These dogs lose their working capabilities when only bred for today's show ring and primarily for looks. On the flip side, the "American Field Lab" has been bred to endure 400 to 500-yard retrieves afield in highly competitive sporting tests, requiring longer legs for running, finer bones, a thinner coat, and a much sleeker body structure. These dogs are brilliant, problem-solving machines who thrive to run hard and work. Both of these Labrador Retriever varieties have significantly veered away from the historical development of the breed, and they continue to evolve and morph with the changing expectations of judging practices. This story is consistent across many breeds that were historically bred for a purpose and temperament that supported that purpose.

Here's another example: the Old English Bulldog was initially bred in England hundreds of years ago for bull baiting. Over centuries, these dogs developed stocky bodies, massive jaws, and a ferocious and savage temperament. These dogs were expected to attack a tethered bull, grabbing it by the nose and pinning it to the ground. After bull baiting was banned in 1835, around 1874, with the registration of this breed, a new standard began to develop. While today's bulldogs look tough, they have been bred to be calmer and less aggressive. But consider their history! You cannot take that 'bull' attacking attitude out of this dog. They have incredible intestinal fortitude. Read about them now, according to the AKC, and you might get a false sense of security that today's breeders have entirely removed aggression. The Old English Bulldog is an intensely bred athletic dog.

Take some time to review how to read an AKC Pedigree. There you will find important background information for you to be aware of with your breeder and future purebred.

Even with meticulous breeding practices, achieving 100% health in puppies cannot be guaranteed. Nonetheless, reputable breeders prioritize the well-being of their pups and provide support for addressing serious health concerns. Typically, breeders establish comprehensive contracts to outline such provisions. Additionally, they may restrict breeding rights by offering pups with limited registration, preventing buyers from breeding the dog, or registering litters with organizations like the AKC. These measures serve to safeguard the integrity of the breeder's bloodlines.

To Breed or Not to Breed

I am often amazed at how many people check off on our QK Canine Training Assessment Form that they want to breed their dog! Owners are typically THRILLED with their dogs that they got from stellar genetics, so now they suddenly feel that they, too, should pass on their dog's traits. These owners need to fully comprehend the work, integrity, and dedication that created their dog in the first place. Unless this puppy owner has done due diligence to fully health test their adult dog AND make efforts to prove the dog's pedigree through temperament, intelligence, performance, or conformation shows, then you are only doing a disservice to the breed.

If you want a dog as stellar as the one you own, go back to your breeder or similar genetics! Each time an inexperienced puppy owner thinks it is a good idea to reproduce their dog, it typically is the beginning of problems getting intertwined into the breed. And consider this: even reputable breeders may have trouble finding the best homes for their beloved puppies.

When these 'backyard litters' are produced by inexperienced owners of excellent dogs, they often breed to keep a puppy, with little realization of the consequence that it takes a ton of work to properly whelp a litter of puppies, let alone the enormous task to safely and responsibly sell the other puppies. And so begins the downward spiral of those stellar genetics!

FINDING THE RIGHT BREEDER

Now that you've selected the breed or mix for all the right reasons, how do you find a good breeder (should you choose this route)? It can be beneficial to go to the AKC website and look up specific Breed Parent Clubs (i.e., German Shorthaired Club of America) to learn about their recommended and screened breeders, including those who accomplish Canine Health Information Center (CHIC) testing for their breed. Remember that while CHIC tests do not guarantee a perfectly healthy puppy, the due diligence a breeder performs to rule out genetic predispositions to diseases helps minimize the risks.

When you locate breeders, be prepared that a quality breeder will interview you as much as you inquire about them and their puppies. Ask questions! Learn how to read a pedigree. A pedigree can show their dog's lineage and the notable titles the dogs have achieved. There are also titles from other organizations such as UKC, NAVHDA, HRC, NASDA, and many more based on your geographic location.

These titles are proof that, before a judge's eye, based on specific criteria or a system, a dog passes a test or places in a competition to achieve a permanent title reflective of conformational breed standards (looks, physiology) or tests based on intelligence or ability to perform tasks to challenge that individual breed (herding, sporting, field, agility, obedience, scent work, etc.). Titles further validate that a dog can meet the breed's standard by physiology, intelligence, athleticism, trainability, and workability. Therefore, the more titles in a pedigree, the more you can see that a breeder was striving to breed proven titled dogs that have been thoughtfully, methodically, and carefully trained and campaigned to prove their value and abilities.

In layperson's terms, if you want a calmer Labrador Retriever as a family companion, do not buy an intensely bred field dog loaded with FCs and AFCs in its pedigree. That shows a super athletic, intelligent, and driven work animal who will not thrive in a more sedentary household. Those dogs are super athletes who want to chase, run, problem-solve, and work.

Conversely, if you want a Labrador to be your next field dog, a pedigree with all CH show titles (or no titles) will not necessarily get you the athlete you may need for hours upon hours of hunting or a dog with adequate prey drive. Do your research and understand pedigrees!

What if you want a companion pug? This brachycephalic breed, characterized by its shortened head, short nose, and flat face, often suffers from airway issues due to its breeding for the popular 'flat face' appearance. These breeds have many health issues, including dental, breathing, and eye problems. In this case, it would be most beneficial to research breeders who health test these breeds and show these dogs for conformation. The breed standards may help you pursue more conformational correctness. If dogs in their lineage are also titled in sporting events, they may be healthier in the long run! This is because these dogs have demonstrated a physical element of performance capability.

QUALITIES OF A GOOD BREEDER

Qualities of a good breeder often include a detailed interview process. The breeder typically provides a written contract and offers a health guarantee. They may only sell their dogs with AKC Limited Registration, which means you do not have their permission to breed this dog, and you cannot register a litter from it. Breeders often have their puppies examined by a veterinarian to rule out obvious heart issues and perform an overall wellness exam, which includes checking the eyes, teeth, palate, appearance, lungs, and genital areas (ensuring both testicles are present or assessing the vulva).

Puppies will have received deworming and their first round of vaccines. The first 7 to 8 weeks of a puppy's life with the breeder involve dedication, hard work, and early preparation to handle, socialize, and keep the pups happy and healthy. Breeders may allow you to visit once the pups reach five weeks of age, and they will better understand each pup's personality, allowing them to guide you toward the best match. You can also assess the pup's living conditions for cleanliness in the breeder's home or kennel and view the entire litter and the dam.

SECTION TWO
PREPPING FOR HOMECOMING

Puppy Arrival Checklist

It's advisable to schedule a wellness exam within 48 hours of bringing your new puppy home. The minute you are approved and have decided to move forward, get on your vet's calendar as the wait can sometimes be weeks or months. Even if the breeder's vet has previously examined the puppy, this proactive visit serves several vital purposes. Your vet will independently examine your pup and check the heart and lungs for serious issues again. It's best to know right away if there are any significant health concerns so you don't get too attached only to find out later your pup has a heart murmur or recognizable disease. The vet can also collect a stool sample because nearly half of all puppies pick up parasites (worms, coccidia, or giardia).

Vaccinations: Puppies typically receive three rounds of puppy vaccines starting after six weeks of age. Before that, they still have antibodies from their mother. The puppy vaccines may start in weeks six to eight, so your breeder may have given them their first round. After that, they repeat every four to six weeks until your pup reaches about 16 weeks of age.

The core vaccines recommended for most puppies include distemper, adenovirus, parvovirus, and rabies, most often required by law for pups 16 weeks. Non-core vaccines may only be recommended based on your dog's exposure to geographical areas or how frequently they will contact other dogs in boarding, public parks, or high-traffic dog areas. These include Leptospira (a deadly bacteria found in soil and water), Bordetella bronchiectasis (canine cough), Canine parainfluenza, Borrelia burgdorferi (Lyme Disease), Influenza (H3N8 and H3N2), and Rattlesnake vaccine. There could be others based on your region.

Consult with your vet about which non-core vaccines are most appropriate based on where you live and what your pup may be exposed to. Are you in the woods? Near a lake? Around a great deal of wildlife? Once pups receive their initial vaccines, they will receive boosters every one to three years based on the dosage requirements.

Puppies put everything in their mouths, including their feet, making them susceptible to parasites, infections, or exposure due to their delicate immune systems. Regular stool samples during the first few months are essential for appropriate treatment. Additionally, starting a relationship with your veterinarian right away is beneficial. They can meet your pup and be available in case of emergencies or if you have any concerns. During the initial wellness check, your pup might not need their next round of puppy shots. However, consider this time and money well spent for your pup's future health and to build a relationship with your veterinarian.

Health Insurance: Pursuing health insurance for your puppy is a GREAT idea! Do it now, and don't delay. My choice is

Healthy Paws Pet Insurance, and their link is https://www. healthypawspetinsurance.com. Even my veterinarian friends have their dogs on health insurance policies. Many options are available, and today, your general practice veterinarian most often refers you to a specialist who can be extremely expensive. These health insurance policies can assist with all aspects of your dog's wellness and care from accidents, injuries, and illnesses. They are extremely valuable for diagnostic care, surgeries, dermatology issues, and post-surgical rehabilitation and can even cover cancer treatment. There are many options, so look into them to see which ones work best for your dog, geographic area, and coverage options.

I could not be happier with the health insurance for my dogs. All of my dogs are insured. Sadly, their health insurance is way more cost-effective and comprehensive than ours! I consider the feeding, training, veterinary wellness exams, vaccines, and preventative medications part of the financial responsibility for owning a dog. Pet health insurance is the peace of mind and the ability to choose the best care for accidents, illnesses, and injuries.

These are stressful times when you need to see specialists, and isn't it great comfort knowing you can pursue some of the best specialists available and say YES to all of the tests required to diagnose and treat your beloved pet in the face of sickness and emergencies? It is best to immediately buy a policy with your new puppy and keep them insured throughout their lives. I am confident that you will not regret this decision.

A typical hospital bill will run over $1500 daily, and knee surgeries start at $3500. These insurances can even cover rehabilitation for post and pre-surgical care and treatments, medications, and much more, with rates as low as $50 to $75 per month based on your dog's age, breed, and geographic location.

Puppy Shopping List

Crate: An enclosed crate, preferably a molded plastic one like the Vari Kennel brand, is an essential training tool. This crate provides safe confinement for your pup and creates a den-like environment, thanks to its closed sides. In contrast, wire crates need 360-degree shelter, so covering them with a blanket might not be as effective. Additionally, wire crates can bend, collapse, and pose risks to pups determined to escape. Imagine having a bedroom with glass walls and no sense of protection – it's not ideal.

Bedding: For crate bedding, a plain fleece mat is an excellent choice. Avoid towels, as pups can pull apart terry cloth string loops and ingest them, leading to potential problems. Steer clear of bedding with piped edges, zippers, or stuffing, as pups tend to chew on these items. The golden rule is to remove any bed that your pup starts to chew on. No bed at all is better than having to remove one that causes an intestinal blockage surgically!

Toys: When shopping for toys and chew bones, ensure they are age and size-appropriate for your pup and do not pose choking hazards. Soft or plush toys should only be used during supervised play. Unsupervised toys may include yak chew bones, Kongs, or toys that encourage chewing but are safe if ingested. All puppies want to chew, so finding them safe chew toys helps to satiate that carnal desire directed towards something that is theirs rather than your woodwork or furniture.

Grooming Supplies and Schedule: Remember grooming equipment, including brushes, ear and eye wipes, puppy shampoos, towels or a shammy for drying, and nail clippers, along with a Dremel tool. Start massaging the pup's feet so they are comfortable during nail clipping. Puppy nails are sharp and can cause much damage if not filed down.

Nail Care: Begin with repetitive nail care when they are puppies. Please don't ignore this! And take them to a local groomer if you need help. Nails should be maintained weekly with growing pups and at least once a month and often twice with some adult dogs. Start this routine early since puppy nails, like their teeth, are like little needles and can cause a lot of tears to your skin.

One of dog care's most crucial yet often overlooked aspects revolves around their nails. Ensuring your pup's future health and well-being requires proactive nail care. Begin by gently touching their feet daily, firmly but kindly. It's essential to persist, as resistance should not be an option. Gradually progress to handling each foot, toe, and nail.

Introduce the use of an emery board or nail file to acclimate them to the peculiar sensation of nail maintenance. While filing may yield little results initially, the objective is to establish a foundation for accepting foot handling and nail care. This exercise should become a daily routine.

Transition to a pair of high-quality dog nail clippers, trimming just the tips of their nails. Consistency is vital, and incorporating these steps into your daily interactions will contribute to a positive nail care experience for your furry friend.

"I'm afraid to hit their quick" or "They hate their nails cut" is not an excuse for nail neglect in dogs. If you need more confidence trimming or filing their nails, take them to a local groomer or pet supply store. Your vet tech will also offer to trim down their nails when they are at their scheduled appointments.

The moment you hear a click-click on the floor, your dog's nails are putting pressure on the back of their nail bed, and this causes pain. They shift their weight back onto their heels, their toes become elongated or deformed, and this change in stance to avoid pain soon affects their elbows, shoulders, neck, spine, and entire movement. Don't let this happen to your dog!

Bathing: Puppies should receive baths regularly. First and foremost, bathe the pup anytime it may soil itself or its crate. A clean pup will work harder to stay clean, whereas a pup allowed to be messy or lie in its filth will often be more prone to messing in the crate. They can accept just being smelly and yucky.

Use your kitchen sink, warm water, and puppy-specific shampoo when the pup is tiny. Use a cotton ball to wipe out their ears, as pups get filthy ears. For any breed that requires professional grooming, with longer coats or hair that continuously grows, it is critical to start them very young with a groomer.

Good groomers help puppies learn to stand still safely and accept the grooming table and the scissors, clippers, and brushes. They make it a pleasant experience so the puppy learns to patiently endure the rigors of grooming. Owning a long-haired pup and not performing regular grooming to maintain a healthy coat is cruel and unfair. Long hair can mat and tangle easily, and these mats are very painful. They can cause severe skin irritations and only worsen when neglected. Your pup should be fully vaccinated before going to a groomer or a public do-it-yourself dog wash facility.

Cleaning Supplies: Lastly, have some cleaners on hand for those inevitable puppy messes. Products like Simple Green Cleaner, OdoBan, or non-toxic pet-safe cleaners can be helpful.

Food and Supplements: Be consistent with your pup's diet, ideally keeping them on the diet they came with initially. If you plan to change their diet, do so gradually over a few weeks to avoid upsetting their gastrointestinal system. Ensure that the diet is tailored to your pup's specific breed needs, as a balanced diet is crucial for their growth and development. Puppy food is specifically balanced with calcium, fat, and protein to help with your pup's growth based on toy breeds, regular, large, or giant-sized breeds. The goal is to provide sufficient nutrients to help best support your pup's physical and cognitive health.

Choose love with leadership over indulgence in food. Obesity can shorten a dog's lifespan by an average of 2.5 years, causing strain on joints, fatty tumors, and an increased risk of sports injuries. Show your love through regular exercise and mental challenges rather than relying on endless treats. Prioritize their well-being for a longer, happier life.

Consider using supplements to support your pup's joint health, provide pro and prebiotics for their gut health, and boost their immune system and overall well-being. Supplements can also be beneficial in preventing illnesses and allergies, and some, like Omega supplements, can improve skin, coat health, and cognitive development.

We have created an excellent line of supplements (Devotion) for complete care, joint support, digestive wellness, immune support, and more! Please check out the Resources section in the back of this book for more information.

Puppy ID Collar: While a fashionable embroidered collar with your pup's name may look cute, consider the primary purpose of an ID collar. It's essential that anyone who finds your lost pup can identify them and contact you promptly. Opt for a bold statement on a pop riveted ID collar that includes the word "REWARD" and your contact information. In emergencies, this can be a lifesaver. Additionally, a belt buckle-style collar with an adjustable fit and a brass ID plate is a practical choice. It's waterproof, minimizing bacterial growth from staying wet, and it doesn't create annoying clanging and dangling sounds.

Your dog gets loose and is hit by a car. Do you want the person first on the scene to read 'REWARD Owner's Name' with two best phone numbers, or 'Hi, My name is Fluffy'?

Worse yet, no collar at all!?

While a microchip is excellent for helping identify a lost dog, it will not help in a life-and-death emergency.

Years ago, we found a Golden Retriever hit by a car. The dog was in dire need of help.

Thankfully, she had an ID collar, and while we were rushing her to the nearest vet to save her life, I was able to reach the owner, who met us there and was able to approve lifesaving care for this dog. Had there been no ID collar, a vet typically cannot just help to treat or save a dog's life without a commitment to payment for their services. It was not my responsibility or place to make lifesaving decisions for this dog or to post my credit card to cover this (although, as an animal lover, I most likely would have!) Clearly identifying emergency contact numbers can mean the difference, so utilize the space on your dog's collar for important contact information rather than your dog's name.

Puppy Gates: If you have an open floor plan and need to restrict your pup's movement during their early stages, consider using puppy gates to section off areas like the kitchen or a smaller room. Alternatively, you can use an EX or exercise pen to create a gaited enclosure if you have an open floor plan. While most puppies feel insecure and abandoned if left in these pens alone, they make an interactive play area and help confine pup safely under your watchful eye.

15-Foot Cotton Leash: A 15-foot cotton leash is a versatile tool. It can be used for walks, allowing your pup to wander and go to the bathroom. Indoors, it helps keep your pup under supervision and reinforces recall training.

Even buying an inexpensive 50-foot cotton clothesline and cutting it into various lengths is a valuable tool to help you keep control of your pup, nurture appropriate behavior by always being hands-on, and discourage games of keep away or chase me.

Planning for How your Pup will Arrive

Road Trip: Consider personally picking up your puppy as it can be a great and uncomplicated option. Ensure you have a travel-safe plastic crate properly secured in your vehicle to prevent it from moving or flipping. When taking rest stops, avoid public areas, dog parks, or places with other dogs, as your new puppy may not have received full vaccinations yet. Opt for off-the-beaten-path grassy areas for walks and potty breaks. Keep your pup on a leash at all times and closely supervise them to prevent them from picking up anything they shouldn't.

Helpful tip: Be prepared for any crate mess by bringing extra bedding and cleaning supplies, such as plastic bags, paper towels, and non-toxic cleaner.

Airline: Flying a puppy from the breeder is another option, but it can have specific limitations depending on the airline. Each airline may have age restrictions, size limits, and temperature constraints for transporting dogs. Puppies can be safely shipped in cargo within temperature guidelines, which can be efficient for long-distance trips. Alternatively, you can bring your puppy with you as a carry-on, and most airlines are accommodating in such cases. However, it's crucial to thoroughly research each airline's specific regulations regarding puppy travel, and you often need a state-licensed veterinary health certificate when flying with your pup.

Private Shipper/Nanny: Consider using a pet nanny or private shipper to transport your puppy by airline, train, or roadways. These individuals and services can provide a safe and efficient way to receive your new pup. There are numerous private shippers available, ranging from single-pet transport to multiple dogs with multiple destinations and stops along the route. It's essential to conduct due diligence by checking backgrounds and asking for referrals to ensure you choose a reputable source for this transportation service.

Appropriate Age of Puppy at Arrival

Now, consider the appropriate age to get a puppy, weighing the pros and cons. Most breeders allow new owners to adopt their puppies at 7 to 8 weeks old. While some studies suggest that 49 days is the optimal time to bring your pup home, there are advantages and disadvantages to getting a puppy earlier or later.

Puppies should ideally stay with their littermates until they are at least seven weeks old. During this time, they benefit significantly regarding their development, safety, and understanding of pack structure. Puppies become mobile and active around three weeks of age. Over the entire seven weeks, they gain valuable experiences from their littermates.

Now, let's explore why seven to eight weeks is the optimum time. By seven weeks, puppies' personalities shine, making it easier to identify the boldest and most reserved individuals. Breeders often notice these traits from early behaviors, such as the pup who consistently nurses first or who's always at the top of the pile. Separating the pups at this stage allows their distinct personalities to flourish.

Around seven weeks, pups also begin forming pack structures. Sometimes, larger pups may dominate smaller ones, and you might observe pups ganging up on each other. Rather than allowing such early bullying to occur, separating the pups at this age enables their characteristics to emerge.

It's worth noting that puppies who remain with a breeder or in a kennel, cage, or pet store for 3 to 4 months may develop early habits that can be challenging to break later on. However, some breeders keep pups even longer to monitor their development closely and select those that best represent their breeding program. Many breeders will keep a few puppies out of their litter, which may be their top picks for their future breeding program.

At just seven weeks, it is difficult to determine which pup may be the best choice regarding temperament, size, bone structure, eye color, movement, attitude, intelligence, and more.

Breeders strive to pick out the best combination resulting from the mating of the sire and dam to help carry on their breeding program.

I have purchased pups four to six months old from breeders that were kept as future breeding dogs but later were not ideal for their breeding program. These pups often were fantastic choices since their breeder worked on crate and house training, manners, and socialization. This scenario may be an option, and when you reach out to a breeder, they may tell you about a puppy they kept but decided to sell. This is great for some folks who do not have the time or experience to endure the very earliest puppyhood training, ages two to three months.

SECTION THREE
WELCOME HOME

Two to Four Months

It's time! You've done your research, homework, and shopping, and now it's finally time to bring home your newest pack member! The weeks between two to four months encompass a critical time. The foundations formed during these weeks will set the tone and relationship for years to come. As such, we'll cover this incredible period's overarching goals and milestones.

During this early phase of a puppy's life, you have a unique opportunity to shape them into a well-behaved citizen and prepare them for training. Essentially, you're teaching the puppy how to learn. While puppies are undeniably adorable, it's crucial to establish yourself as the leader during this time.

The puppy-rearing process and methodology outlined below provide a structured routine. It explains why strict rules and structure are essential and draws from 30 years of experience successfully raising puppies that lead stable and fulfilling lives. ***The guiding principle is, "If you don't want the adult dog to do it, don't let the puppy do it."*** Each step in the puppy-rearing process is carefully nurtured, listed, and explained for a specific purpose.

The ultimate goal is to mold, guide, shape, nurture, and create a wonderful puppy willing and eager to undergo training. Conversely, if a puppy is spoiled early on and learns to be messy, noisy, demanding, incessant, needy, or unruly, it may never reach its full potential.

"We're not training puppies; we're creating behavioral patterns." Rick Smith, trainer, clinician, competitor, breeder, writer, American Brittany Club Hall of Fame inductee, and current (2023) President of Bird Dog Foundation, Inc.

Schedule

When you first bring your puppy home, establishing a schedule is crucial for effectively managing nighttime sleep, feeding, and house training. This schedule involves the following: sleep, eat, walk, potty, bonding, sleep, eat, potty, play, sleep, and repeat! During those initial weeks, creating a routine and maintaining consistency is critical. Your role is to assist in shaping a puppy that learns to switch off when needed and sleeps uninterrupted and adequately (which is upwards of 18 to 20 hours a day!), eats with purpose, and comprehends that outdoor elimination is the norm.

Here are some key takeaways:

- Routine and Consistency: The puppy's most significant need is a routine and your unwavering consistency in following it.

- Molding and Shaping Behaviors: Your actions and the routine you establish help mold and shape the puppy's behaviors.

The Need for Sleep: They say a tired dog is a happy dog, but this is not true for a pup. Many people underestimate the need for puppies to have 18 to 20 hours of sleep between birth and four months. This extensive sleep is essential because puppies grow to nearly adult size in their first six months, and their rapidly developing brains and bodies require ample rest to support this rapid growth.

To put it in perspective, humans take nearly 18 years to reach full maturity. One of the most significant mistakes people make is overstimulating their puppies and depriving them of vital sleep time. Puppies denied sufficient sleep can develop behavioral issues, including emotional instability, overreactions, mood swings, aggression, anxiety, and more. Such puppies may also never learn to switch off, becoming incessantly active, anxious, and possibly neurotic.

I can envision it now. All the naysayers say, "There is no way a puppy will sleep that much!" "My puppy would NEVER sleep that much!" Ok then, how many puppies have you raised?

Did you genuinely raise them, or did they raise you? Did you nurture and satisfy their demands, creating little monsters? I have whelped over a dozen litters from my breeding stock of Labrador Retrievers and German Shorthaired Pointers, and I have helped, raised, and trained hundreds of puppies of various breeds for myself and my clients. Walks to drain energy, thoughtful and purposeful interactions to shape behavior, and crate time are the recipes for a successful outcome.

Even if a pup is simply awake in its crate, they are learning patience, manners, and self-control. Clients often explain their pup's behavior in the evening with their 'witching hour,' an intense desire to bite, and having a high level of crazed energy. Often, those are pups that have been overstimulated and are overtired!

Embracing the Canine Fairy Godmother: The Enchanting Retreat in the Crate

Imagine a magical scene where your Fairy Godmother, with a graceful wave of her wand, presents you with an umbrella cocktail and invites you to recline in a hammock with your favorite book. That's the enchantment we strive for in the crate experience. The crate metamorphoses into a haven of serenity and joy in our canine world. It transcends mere confinement; it becomes a sanctuary.

This chapter in the grand story of crate training isn't just about limits; it's about crafting a haven where your pup, guided by their Fairy Godmother (you!), discovers not just a dining space but a realm of tranquility. The Fairy Godmother's spell weaves comfort, calmness, composure, and canine contentment within the crate.

Here are additional safety considerations for puppies under six months:

Supervision and Protection: Puppies under six months require constant care and supervision due to the various dangers that can threaten them. Two common causes of puppy illness, injury, or death include access to electrical cords and ingesting foreign objects that can lead to intestinal blockages, poisoning, or infection.

Many years ago, my seven-week-old puppy had just arrived by plane, and I planned some time away for a week to bond with her. We socialized and visited with my family. She spent time by the pool at my brother's home and met several new people. The next day, while I was seeing friends, my Dad called in a panic, explaining that she was having a seizure! I rushed home, and sure enough, she again presented a seizure, and we rushed her to a local vet. I called her breeder (a notable and longtime producer of this breed), and he said none of his dogs ever had epilepsy. He suggested that I have the pup put down, and he would replace her.

I was devastated! I called my trusted vet back home, and he explained that a 7 to 8-week-old puppy typically does not present with epilepsy that young; she must have gotten into something! Upon a quick investigation, I contacted my brother to ask if he had any chemicals around, only to find out that he had just put down grub poisoning around his pool. Upon reading the ingredients, there was a warning about ingesting. My puppy's life was spared due to some quick thinking and diligence.

On the one hand, I certainly would
not have wanted to euthanize my
new puppy, but to think of the alternative
where I could fall in love with this pup
only to have her become very sickly
would also have been heartbreaking.
That pup went on to receive her AKC
Conformation Champion, Master Hunter,
and NAVHDA Versatile Champion to
become quite an ambassador for her breed.
The moral of the story is that puppies eat
ANYTHING! You must always watch them.

Interactions with Adult Dogs: While adult dogs can serve as valuable mentors to young pups, not all adult dogs have the patience to tolerate rude or obnoxious puppy behaviors. Puppies may jump in an adult dog's face, nip, or attempt to nurse, behaviors that can provoke harsh reactions from adult dogs. These interactions can be harmful or even fatal for the puppy. It's crucial to avoid situations where your young pup is subjected to an intolerant adult dog's responses. While these are often well-deserved corrections, they may be dangerous for young puppies, both physically and emotionally.

Potential Human Risks: Puppies often get underfoot, creating a risk of tripping and accidentally stepping on them. A puppy can easily suffer a broken leg if stepped on.

Additionally, people may unintentionally drop puppies while holding and cuddling them. To mitigate these risks, it's advisable for people, especially children, to sit down or get down on the floor to interact with squirmy puppies safely.

How do you safely pick up a puppy? Humans have ball and socket shoulder joints. Dogs have shoulder blades. You can scoop a child up under the armpits, but doing this action to a puppy forces their shoulder blades outward. Try bending your elbow backward!? Instead, handle a young pup by lifting them by the neck scruff, then quickly supporting their bottom. Hold them securely against your body with your other hand. Do not just support them under their rib cage as you will hear them huff and puff for air as you are squeezing their lungs, making it hard to breathe.

Do not let young children grab the puppies around their middles and let them dangle. Learn to pick up, hold, and support pups safely and successfully: scruff, butt, then secure against your chest. Use two hands, one to keep under the butt, the other supporting against the shoulder area and your body.

Additionally, if a pup decides to squirm and have a meltdown while you are holding him, do not let this behavior enable the pup to win and be put back down. This handling is an early part of patience and tolerance training, which later helps with vet exams, tolerance to nail cutting, and more. When a pup demands to be put down, use gentle pressure to secure and wait them out. Get ready. This interaction can sometimes be an early battle, but it is essential! The moment that they exhale and subdue, you relax.

Teach them that a temper tantrum, struggle, or vocalization will not let them win. Put them back on the floor only when they relax and accept your holding. When you do put them down, do it methodically by allowing their hind feet to touch first. They typically want to bolt as soon as their hind feet touch. Continue to gently hold on until they relax, allow their front feet to touch the ground, pause until they comply with your terms, and then gently let them go.

This simple practice helps to mold and create a more tolerant, trusting, and obedient pup.

The Crate

I'm spending a lot of time on the reasoning behind the crate and why it is essential to raise a proper pup. But first, I want to share with you a mistake we made with my first dog, Ginger, who started it all for me, the one I dedicated this book to.

When we got Ginger, we were once those clueless first-time dog owners who believed crates were cruel. We opted for a puppy gate to confine her in our family room. Unfortunately, Ginger developed severe separation anxiety, leading to destructive chewing—she even chewed our 1970s orange tapestry couch down to the wood frame.

Looking back, I regret that Ginger had to endure our ignorance. She wasn't seeking revenge; she was in a complete state of panic, akin to a baby rocking themselves and sucking their thumbs in stress. She

knew she couldn't protect the entire house,
so she chewed desperately to soothe
her fear and feelings of insecurity.

Comparing it to leaving a toddler home alone, we now under-stand the importance of protecting puppies. Despite their appearance, a 6-month-old pup is more like a 6-year-old child, needing safety, security, and protection. Puppies aren't responsible for managing the home; they're babies.

The crate emerges as the most responsible, kind, and humane way to contain a dog safely. It becomes their den, a source of protection where they can relax. Incorporate dog-safe chew toys or bones, and your home stays safe. It's a crucial tool for managing a puppy's environment and providing peace of mind for the dog and your home.

Because of what I've lived and experienced in my thirty years of working with dogs, the importance of a crate in puppy training cannot be overstated. It serves as a secure and essential tool in the successful and easier rearing of puppies for various reasons. Here's why crate training is crucial:

- **Natural Instincts:** In the wild, expecting canine moth-ers don't leave their vulnerable pups out in the open or unprotected when they venture out to feed or take a break. They seek shelter, often digging dens to pro-vide a secure environment for giving birth and rais-ing their young. Domesticated house dogs share this natural desire to nest, den, and hide to care for their pups safely.

- **Safety and Security:** Puppies instinctively seek safety and security in a den-like environment. Just as you find safety and comfort in your home or that cozy feeling in your bed, puppies feel secure in an enclosed space. During the first four weeks of life, pups sleep, feed, play, and eliminate in this space while their mother diligently cleans up after them while still nursing them.
- **Transition from Litter:** Puppies raised by breeders typically start to eat solid food around four weeks of age as their mother begins to wean them. Even as they start to eat solid food, they continue to find safety and comfort within the confines of their littermates and the enclosed area they share as a pack.
- **Emotional Well-Being:** The transition from their littermates' familiar and safe environment to a new home can be one of the most stressful times in a puppy's life. Being suddenly separated from their pack and feeling alone can cause anxiety and fear.

The crate becomes a crucial tool when you bring a young pup home at around seven to eight weeks or older. While crate training may take some time and patience to master, it will ultimately provide comfort and security for your puppy.

Crate training is a fundamental aspect of raising a well-behaved and balanced puppy. It sets the stage for many aspects of your dog's life, including their ability to relax, follow rules, and handle confinement when necessary.

Here are some key points and insights into successful crate training:

Understanding the Puppy's Perspective: When introducing your puppy to the crate, they may protest by crying, whining, or trying to escape. This response is perfectly normal and part of the process. It's essential to recognize that early crate training is a valuable lesson in patience and self-control for your pup. It's an opportunity to teach them that such behavior will not lead to attention, freedom, or having things their way.

The Chess Game of Crate Training: Crate training involves establishing a hierarchy of rules and boundaries. It's like a game of chess between you and your puppy. If you succeed in this game, you create a patient, accepting, and well-behaved dog that can handle confinement and downtime, making it adaptable to various situations.

The Alternative Outcome: Puppy owners who refuse to crate train or give up on it early may face different outcomes. Puppies not taught to accept rules, downtime, and confinement may develop anxiety when left alone, fail to engage an "off" switch, and become destructive. These pups might struggle with anxiety and behavior issues because they were not allowed to learn to relax in an enclosed space.

The most common explanation clients give for their pup's crating routine is that they crate overnight and when they leave home. Then, throughout the day, these pups roam freely, sleep at their owners' feet, and enjoy total freedom while their owners are around. While the owner feels this is successful, the pup often does not sleep soundly. Your puppy is frequently under-foot when you move about your house. They effectively follow your every move, owning, guarding, and shadowing you.

In their mind, they are your partner and become attached to your every move. This constant interruption certainly makes for much-interrupted sleep! While you may have success over-night since your pup still can keep an eye on you, leaving home while you crate your pup often leads to what people call 'sep-aration anxiety.' You have created a pup codependent on your presence, and your dog is now fearful, insecure, or all-out angry that you left him behind! He typically owns YOU; now you are suddenly calling the shots when you leave? How about you show ownership and leadership of yourself and your home and crate puppy during ALL his naps while you are home?!

This consistency reinforces that you will live as usual in your home. During those critical months when pups need 18 to 20 hours of uninterrupted sleep, they can sleep peacefully once they realize they are not your consummate shadow. Please don't create a codependent puppy; they will forever suffer a life of anxiety and distress all because you thought it was cruel to crate them and you did not have the education, foresight, or self-discipline to do what is best for their needs. Imagine your own life if you always needed someone with you!?

Baseline Rules: Establishing some baseline rules is crucial. One fundamental rule is that puppies always sleep in their crates. Since puppies need a substantial amount of sleep (around 18 to 20 hours a day), they spend much time in their crates. Feeding them in their crates also helps build a positive association with the space.

Feeding in the Crate: Feeding your puppy in their crate has several benefits. Puppies quickly learn to associate their crates with food, providing a safe space to eat without distractions. It can also help prevent food-guarding behavior (especially in the presence of other dogs around) and encourages them to eat their meals with conviction, leading to a healthier eating routine.

When done correctly, crate training creates a safe and secure space for your puppy, promotes self-control and patience, and sets the foundation for a well-mannered and balanced adult dog.

The guidelines provided are essential for successful crate training and ensuring the safety and well-being of your puppy. Let's break down the do's and don'ts:

Crate Dos:

- Use an Enclosed Plastic Crate: An enclosed plastic crate provides your puppy with a secure and den-like environment.
- Use the Crate for Naps and Sleep: Establish the crate as the go-to spot for all naptime and overnight sleep.
- Passive Downtime in the Crate: Encourage passive downtime in the crate to help your puppy learn to relax.
- Crate for Car Travel: Use the crate for safe car travel, ensuring your puppy is secured during rides. This consistency even helps with travel sickness as pups feel secure in their crate. It is a stable, comfortable, and consistent environment.
- Allow bedding (but Be Cautious): While you can provide bedding, monitor your puppy's behavior to ensure they don't chew or ingest it.

- Keep the Crate Clean: Clean the crate promptly if your puppy has an accident inside.
- Feeding in the Crate: Serve all meals inside the crate to create positive associations.
- Provide Access to Water Outside of the Crate: Keep fresh water available for your puppy outside the crate.
- Puppies drink a lot and need water.
- Offer water any time you take them out of their crate.
- Do not withhold water consumption; manage it around their bathroom schedule.
- Offer Safe Chew Bones: Place safe chew bones inside the crate for entertainment.
- Teach the "Crate" Command: Train your puppy to enter the crate on command and wait inside until you release them. This command is the early start for their GO and COME commands!

Crate Don'ts:

- Avoid Wire Crates Initially: Wire crates may not give a young puppy the same sense of security. Enclosed plastic crates are preferable for early training.
- No Towels in Crates: Avoid using towels as bedding inside the crate, as puppies may chew and ingest them.
- Choose Safe Toys While Crated: Avoid plush toys or any items that could be ingested or pose choking hazards.
- Don't Give In to Whining: Resist the urge to let your puppy out of the crate if they're making noise just to be released.

- Respect Crate Privacy: Ensure that others do not disturb your puppy while they're in the crate. It's their den, and they should have quiet.
- Manage Water Intake: Don't leave water inside the crate; puppies may spill it or drink excessively, leading to frequent urination.
- These guidelines provide a solid framework for effective crate training and creating a safe, comfortable space for your puppy. Following these dos and don'ts will help your puppy adapt to crate living and develop positive associations with their crate.

Common Crate Conundrums And Questions

Shutting the Crate Door: It's essential to close the crate door every time your puppy is inside, whether it willingly goes in or you place it there. This action helps establish the concept of confinement and ensures its safety.

Water in the Crate: While puppies need access to fresh water throughout the day, it's generally best to offer water when you let them out to eliminate. This schedule helps you monitor their water intake and reduce the likelihood of messes in the crate.

Wire Crate vs. Enclosed Crate: Enclosed crates, like plastic ones, are preferable for young puppies as they create a sense of safety and security like a den. Wire crates can be used but require additional measures, such as covering them with a blanket to make a cozier environment. Covering the crate only serves as something to chew on and pull into the crate, and a determined puppy can escape a wire crate, often getting hurt in the process.

Duration of Crate Time: The ideal crate time for a young puppy is up to 8 hours overnight. During the day, crate time should be interspersed with breaks for elimination, play, training, and affection. While there may be times when your puppy needs to spend longer periods in the crate, these should be minimized, and arrangements for bathroom breaks and exercise should be made.

Handling Messes in the Crate: Urination or defecation in the crate can be expected for puppies initially. I call them incidents, not accidents since they most likely will occur! Use a non-toxic cleaner to clean the crate thoroughly and replace any bedding if necessary. If your puppy smells like urine or feces, bathe them. Consistent cleanliness and regular bathroom breaks will help them eventually eliminate outside.

Importantly, avoid scolding your puppy for crate soiling. Instead, focus on maintaining a clean crate, bedding, and puppy. Over time, as your puppy matures and becomes more accustomed to the routine, they will likely learn to control themselves better and willingly eliminate outside. Remove bedding entirely, as some pups can tolerate soiling their bedding and avoid being in their mess. By removing the bedding, a pup has to endure their mess, and they may be much more deterred from that option. Some pups, in general, may take longer to grasp the concept, and you may find yourself cleaning up messes daily. Stay diligent; it WILL get better!!

I have raised pups for myself and clients who have NEVER had one mess in their crates. That is quite an anomaly! Mostly, I expect early messes in a pup's crate and consider it part of the puppy rite of passage. On the flip side, I have also endured marathon crate training where pups messed every day for weeks, if not months. This situation happened two years ago with my own GSP puppy. She had a UTI (urinary tract infection) as a seven-week-old puppy, and from a medical standpoint, she could not hold her urine.

Even after antibiotic treatment, whether it became routine or comfortable, or perhaps her UTI still caused her lack of bladder control, she went nearly two months before she stopped peeing in her crate. In this instance, what began as a health issue either continued or became conditioned for her. She would bark to go out but let loose before I could get to her.

Despite my diligent schedule, it happened every night and even throughout the night. She was quite a fun pup to raise… NOT!

Puppy Barks Incessantly While Crated: Many puppies will bark more during the initial days of crate training as they adjust to a new environment without the company of their littermates. To address incessant barking, you can try the following strategies:

- **Tire Out Your Puppy:** Engage in physical and mental exercises to tire your puppy before crating it. Short walks or interactive play sessions can help; however, brain-engaging exercises drain the mental side and delve into the pup's working and problem-solving mode to satiate and exhaust them.
- **Offer High-Value Chew Items:** Providing a particular chew bone or toy your puppy enjoys can distract and keep them occupied in the crate.
- **Create a Secluded Area:** Place the crate in a quiet and secluded area of your home to minimize external stimuli.
- **Establish a Schedule:** Develop a consistent schedule for crate time and regular potty breaks. A schedule helps prevent your puppy from barking to signal their need to eliminate. While I try to refrain from letting a pup out for barking, if I do have my pup on a schedule but suddenly they are crying or barking, sometimes they really do need to eliminate. Don't get sucked into your pup barking to go out (as this can be a demanding pup pushing you around), but be thoughtful and heed their warnings if emergency potty breaks are needed.
- **Use Corrections:** If the barking persists despite your efforts, consider using gentle corrections. You can shake the crate mildly or use a spray bottle with water to

discourage barking. These corrections should be applied immediately when the barking occurs and are meant to deter the behavior.

Remember that excessive barking must be addressed early to prevent it from becoming a long-term behavior issue. Consistency, positive reinforcement, and moments of correction are essential to successful crate training.

The duration of crate usage can vary significantly from one dog to another and depends on various factors, including the dog's age, maturity, and personality.

Here are some considerations regarding crate usage:

Establishing the Crate as a Positive Space: The primary goal is to create a positive association with the crate as a safe and comfortable den-like space where your dog can relax. This goal applies to all dogs, regardless of age. Crate training should begin early in a puppy's life to help them learn self-control and patience.

Age and Maturity: Young puppies will need to be crated more frequently, especially during house training. You can gradually reduce crate time as they mature and become better behaved. However, adapting the crate schedule to your dog's needs is essential.

Personality and Behavior: A dog's personality plays a significant role. Some dogs may be more relaxed and well-behaved, making it easier to grant them more freedom within the home sooner. Others may be more active, mischievous, or prone to destructive behavior, requiring more extended crate usage. Some dogs thrive best when crated when they cannot be supervised, as long as there is a routine with adequate exercise and enrichment training.

Guarding Behavior: Dogs that exhibit guarding or territorial behavior when left loose in the home may benefit from continued crate usage or specific training to address these behaviors. When left loose in the house, these dogs have made it their sole job to guard, own, and protect their domain. While it is reassuring to know that your dog is your home security system, dogs that choose to bark incessantly, jump up into windows, or pace the home nonstop may ultimately become aggressive (even towards friends and family members) when they practice taking their job that seriously.

Gradual Transition: When considering allowing a dog more freedom in the home, it's advisable to make this transition gradually. Start with short unsupervised time while you are home and progressively increase it as you gain trust in your dog's behavior.

Ongoing Training: Obedience training and reinforcing good behavior are crucial for dogs of all ages. Please continue to work on commands and reinforce positive behaviors, whether your dog is in the crate or outside.

Consultation with a Professional: If you have concerns about your dog's behavior or the timing of transitioning from crate use to more freedom, consider consulting with a professional dog trainer or behaviorist for guidance tailored to your specific situation. Here is the link where you can set a meeting with me via Zoom with Broome: https://qkdogs. com/our-services/zoomwithbroome/

In summary, there is no one-size-fits-all answer to how long you should use a crate for your dog. Your decision should be based on your dog's individual needs and behavior and your level of comfort with their behavior when given more freedom. The crate will remain a valuable tool for providing structure and safety for your dog throughout its life.

The Leash

Introducing a young puppy to a leash and teaching them how to walk on it is essential to their early training and socialization.

Imagine this: My dad, a grown man, spent over three hours trying to catch his 6-month-old standard poodle, Kadey because he thought letting her off-leash for a walk in the woods was a good idea. What followed was a game of keep-away that involved everything from coddling and tempting with food to pleading and even attempting to drive off. Kadey turned it into the best game ever, leading my dad through a rollercoaster of emotions from humor to impatience, anger, frustration, and severe worry.

Even after building a makeshift cattle catch pen, Kadey's love for escaping stuck with her. Despite training, my dad was inconsistent with his reinforcement, so Kadey became a professional evader. The lesson here? Don't let your pup become a 'Kadey'—consistency in training is critical!

Using a soft, long cotton leash can be a helpful tool during this process. Here are some essential points to remember when introducing a puppy to a leash and beginning leash training:

Start Gradually: As mentioned, many puppies are not used to wearing collars or having anything attached to them. Before introducing the leash, begin by allowing your puppy to wear the collar and become accustomed to it. Most puppies scratch a lot at their collar during this process.

Leash as a Tether: Initially, use the leash as a tether while supervising your puppy indoors. This allows them to drag it around and get used to the sensation of having it attached. Even allow the pup to pull a 4 to 6-foot cotton leash under your watchful eye just so they get used to it attached to their neck.

Prevent Biting: Puppies may chew or bite on the leash out of curiosity. If this happens, gently redirect their attention to a toy or treat. A gentle yet effective, well-timed tug on the leash at the moment of the leash biting can also deter a puppy from holding their leash. While this behavior is charming at first, it only turns into a pup wanting to control themselves on the leash and can become quite an evasive tactic when you later work on leash training.

No Pulling: As I've mentioned, avoid harsh pulling on the leash. Instead, let the puppy explore while keeping the leash slack. When they pull too hard out ahead, turn in the opposite direction (turn, tug, and go), and they will redirect to walk with you. You can encourage them to come back to you, and when they do, reward them with praise and the subsequent release of leash pressure.

Practice Recall: The long leash is an excellent tool for practicing recall (coming when called). Allow your puppy to explore while you hold the leash, and then call them back to you. Reward them generously with a calm, reassuring touch and praise or even a small treat when they respond to your recall command.

Safety First: Always supervise your puppy on a leash, especially with a long leash, to prevent accidents, such as the leash getting tangled or caught on objects.

Short Walks: Keep early leash walks short and positive. Allow your puppy to sniff and explore their environment, but maintain leash control. If you walk in a safe area, you can let the pup drag the leash and explore. Typically, a young puppy will shadow you as they are not brave enough to run off.

However, maintain leash control if there are distractions or lurking dangers, and use the long leash to keep the puppy safe. Even when you drop the 15- to 20-foot light cotton rope, catching a 20-foot dragging rope is much easier than an evasive loose puppy. Gradually increase the length of walks as your puppy becomes more accustomed to the leash and capable of longer outings.

Consistency: Be consistent with your training and expectations. Use the same commands and reward systems every time you work with your puppy on leash walking. You are effectively preparing them for leash training, so understand that these early puppy walks are not just free-for-alls. Instead, they are steps leading toward behavior shaping, manners, and future leash obedience. Practice your long-line recalls often to help reinforce this critical command.

Patience: Remember that leash training takes time and patience. Every puppy is different, and some may adapt more quickly than others. Be patient, stay positive, and celebrate your puppy's progress.

By following these guidelines and introducing your puppy to the leash positively and gently, you can help them develop good leash manners and become a well-behaved walking companion.

Choosing the right equipment for leash training is crucial for the safety and comfort of your puppy. Here's a breakdown of some leash alternatives and their considerations:

1. Short Leashes: Short leashes, often called traffic leads, can be helpful for close control in busy areas. However,

they are not ideal for puppies, especially during initial leash training, as they only allow a little freedom of movement. They are too constrictive, and since a young puppy does not yet know how to yield to pressure, they learn to pull more.

2. Retractable Leashes: Retractable leashes can be problematic, especially for puppies. As I've mentioned, they can teach pulling behavior because pulling extends the leash, so they are rewarded for pulling. Additionally, these leashes can become tangled quickly and pose safety risks. They are generally not recommended for puppies, especially during the early stages of leash training.

I genuinely wish that retractable leashes were illegal. I have heard nightmare stories of the cords or nylon straps becoming tangled around human or dog legs only to cut them like a wire. They reward a dog for pulling because you push a button and give them more freedom when they pull and want more leash. It is not a teaching tool. My scary story goes back years ago when I was at a retriever field trial.

I exited a hotel with one of my male Labradors under control on a short leash. In a flash, I look up to hear a woman screaming as her 85+ pound Chesapeake Bay Retriever pulls the retractable leash handle out of her hands, and he is now barreling at us, teeth bared to attack! Here comes this dog full bore with the leash in tow and the bulky handle bouncing like an erratic missile. We managed to survive unscathed, but picture that scene next time you view a dog handler with a dog on a retractable leash!

3. No Pull-Face Halters: While some people succeed with no pull-face halters on dogs, they should be used cautiously. They work by redirecting the dog's head when they pull, which can be uncomfortable. The bridge of a dog's nose is very sensitive (like our own noses), so essentially, you have the power equal to leading a 2000-pound bull by a nose ring. The problem is that people often hold this device too tight, so the dog receives nonstop pressure, which can lead to nose scarring. Again, they can be very effective but are more of a crutch and not truly a training tool.

4. No Pull Harnesses: No pull harnesses vary in design; however, the concept is to put pressure on the dog's shoulders or armpits when they try to pull, potentially causing discomfort or restricting movement to deter them from pulling. These are not the best choice for young puppies, especially large breeds, as they can affect the developing musculoskeletal system.

   According to sports medicine guru Chris Zink, DVM, Ph.D., DACVP, DACVSMR, "No-pull harnesses are detrimental to a dog's structure and gait and are especially inappropriate for canine athletes. These harnesses sit on top of the bicep and supraspinatus tendons, two of the most commonly injured structures in dog's forelimbs." Even without a leash attached, they affect the way a dog moves because due to the pressure asserted by the harness, dogs will bear less weight on their front legs.

   Additionally, with the leash attached, dogs will bear even less weight on the leg on the far side of the person walking. The harness, therefore, affects the gait of the front limbs, restricts a dog's range of motion, and affects their weight distribution as dogs try to evade the pressure of the harness.

5. Regular Harnesses: Standard harnesses distribute force across a dog's chest and shoulders. While they can be a better option for dogs prone to tracheal issues, those with delicate necks or long backs, they can encourage pulling because they don't provide the same level of feedback as a collar. They might be suitable for puppies for short walks, but transitioning to a collar is essential for training in the long run.

6. Prong Collars: Prong collars are designed to apply pressure evenly around the neck when used correctly, and this pressure simulates a bite feeling (each prong segment pinches the neck with the tightness of the collar). However, they should only be used under the guidance of a professional dog trainer who is experienced and can help them fit correctly, as people often have them too tight or too loose. In general, they are not recommended for puppies, as puppies have delicate necks, and the pressure from a prong collar can be excessive. Additionally, most people who use prong collars still hold tight, consistent pressure on the dog's neck, leading to a frustrated dog who cannot seek pressure release. The dog pulls even more and becomes hardened and desensitized to neck pressure.

When choosing leash equipment for a puppy, it's essential to consider their breed, size, and temperament. Additionally, using positive reinforcement training methods alongside the right equipment is crucial for effective leash training. As you continue to read, you will learn new and successful strategies to get started correctly!

SECTION FOUR
EARLY PUPPY MANNERS

Housetraining

First, let's address the first question on every pup owner's mind: how long can they hold it before they go potty?

A simple rule of thumb to consider when your puppy first arrives is a straightforward mathematical equation based on the pup's age. When a puppy is awake and active (out of the crate/bedding/sleep area), an average puppy will urinate normally within time frames based on age. A quick rule of thumb is Age in Months x 10 = the duration when a puppy naturally urinates. So a 2-month-old puppy may quickly and usually piddle every 20 minutes while up and active, outside their crates, actively awake and moving around.

When pups are young, their bladders are small. Each month, as a puppy develops, matures, and grows, this duration can be increased by 10 minutes (3-month pup every 30 minutes, 4-month every 40 minutes) up to 6 months. At 6 months, it is best practice to be proactive and let the puppy out every 60 minutes while they are up and active until they reach at least 8 months or up to a year.

It's not an Accident; It's an Incident!

Twenty minutes fly by quickly, and each indoor urination incident reinforces the puppy's belief that it's acceptable. Instead, be highly proactive! If in doubt, take the puppy out! Do not get sucked into the game of distraction and constant sniffing. Bringing a puppy out to eliminate should be your single-focused goal. You should bring the puppy to the spot where you would prefer them to go. Give them a few minutes to eliminate. If and when they go, associate a command such as "HURRY HURRY" while they are going, and this will ultimately be their cue to potty on command.

If the puppy becomes too distracted, beyond 5 to 10 minutes with no success, bring the puppy back inside and crate them. Doing so is NOT meant to be a punishment. The confinement of the crate is intended to contain them in an area where they are learning bladder/bowel control. Give them another 20 to 30 minutes of crate confinement, and then try bringing them right back outside. This type of focus and due diligence (while time-consuming) helps to set the routine so that when you bring them out, they are to eliminate. If you bring the puppy back inside and they eliminate inside while loose in your home, then this quickly becomes their pattern and habit.

Remember, these are not accidents; they are incidents. The puppy had to go! They need a routine to learn that when brought outside, one of their first tasks is eliminating and not getting redirected to play.

When indoors with a young puppy 2 to 4+ months, all of their time outside the crate must be supervised. Keep them from roaming out of sight on tiled confined areas as they often see the entire area as a place where they can go potty. If you catch a pup in the act of going potty, you can swiftly grab it and bring it outside, perhaps with some slight disappointment in your voice, 'Oh No' as you see them messing. You cannot correct a young pup for messing in the house after it is done; they do not understand. You NEVER should bring them back to a mess and yell at them after the fact! Doing so only causes them more confusion, and they might run off to a more secluded area to eliminate next time. The GOAL is to focus them to eliminate outside, verbally praise the action and name it, and then bring the puppy back indoors for supervised time.

Puppies also typically have a bowel movement 15 to 30 minutes after eating. So, with the routine of eating in their crates, you will quickly learn your individual puppy's elimination needs, and you can bring them right from the crate to the outdoors to eliminate after meals.

Puppy Pads: Puppy pads can be an excellent option for city dwellers facing the challenge of navigating an elevator or stairways every 20 minutes, which can be pretty daunting. These pads can be beneficial during the first 2 to 3 months when puppies need to go outside very frequently. They may also be easiest to use for small-breed puppies.

However, there is a potential issue with puppy pee pads— puppies can learn to play with and shred them. If this happens, you should immediately correct them for this behavior, either verbally with an attention-grabbing guttural tone or with a shake at the scruff. The correction must be enough to deter them from scratching, shredding, or chewing the pad because ingesting it can be harmful. Make it clear that these actions are not allowed. Of course, this can run a fine line of scaring them away from the pads altogether. Be thoughtful with your praise when they are going potty on the pads, and be careful with your corrections.

Puppies can learn to use the pads, and if you have a toy or small breed in an apartment, you may choose to use them throughout the dog's life. However, it's essential to realize that the more a puppy becomes conditioned to using a puppy pad, the more effort you will need to transition them to eliminating outside.

Another valid reason to use pads is that it can be risky to take city pups outside before they are fully vaccinated; keeping them safe and sheltered indoors may be recommended.

Remember that your pup has a very young immune system and only entirely safe from lurking diseases once they complete their puppy vaccination protocol. It is imperative to keep them away from high-traffic areas such as dog walks, rest-stop pet areas, dog parks, or areas where dogs congregate.

Interactions

The next question on every puppy parent's mind is, how do I start preparing them to behave well? *A great rule of thumb is if you don't want them as an adult dog doing an action, don't let the puppy.* While certain behaviors may be manageable for a five-pound fuzzball, remember that what they do now they'll continue to do as they grow. In this section we'll cover behaviors you want to nip in the bud, such as biting, jumping, growling, resource guarding, roughhousing, barking, and whining.

You're in charge now. Don't be fooled by their cuteness! Puppies are remarkably adept at learning rules and manners from a young age. Their mother is often the first to enforce rules, using growls, pinning the pup, and even gentle bites to correct them when they try to nurse when she's done or when needle-sharp-toothed puppies exhibit inappropriate behavior. Witnessing a mother dog with a high-value bone can be a masterclass in puppy discipline regarding her teaching moment with her pups.

My German Shorthaired moms have taught me valuable lessons when interacting with their litters. It may be the German discipline with the cut-and-dry notion because this breed takes nonverbal communication, pack order, and structure to a whole new level compared to my Labradors, who often let their puppies get away with much more shenanigans. With my last litter, I observed first-time Mom Doozy so gently and lovingly interact with her 1,2 and 3-week-old puppies, allowing them to crawl all over her. She was incredibly tolerant of anything they did. However, the lessons began around four weeks as the pups became more mobile, and she started to wean them naturally as we began offering puppy food.

While she let them nurse some, she adamantly let them know when she was done. First, she would jump out of the whelping box, but if they were loose in our puppy room, she would growl, jump away, and finally abruptly pin an unruly pup for not obeying her. NO means NO. The best lesson came when she took her bone, jumped into the whelping box, and schooled her puppies on the art of "This is MY bone, and you are not allowed to have it!" I recall cringing at her taunting lesson and was mildly fearful she could hurt a puppy, but it was one of the most extraordinary lessons. She was 100% in control, and those pups got a power lesson in respect. As the next four weeks progressed, Doozy interacted with her pups with the skill of a Ph.D. professor, coach, and playmate. The silent, often subtle communication and interactions had incredible purpose, intent, and results.

In an ironic twist, four of Doozy's pups visited at one year old, and she maintained total silent control over them. Even after a year apart, they submitted to her authority the moment they approached. While playful and kind, Doozy teased them with toys and play, asserting instant authority and corrections. The pups showed immense respect and a hint of fear. Witnessing her in action was a training day to remember—I still relish the lessons she imparted.

Spending time around older dogs that are excellent with puppies is genuinely enlightening. You'll be amazed at the bonding, mentoring, and lessons. Puppies quickly grasp their boundaries with an older dog. A silent communication system based on body language, teeth displays, growls, sudden lunges, and gentle but assertive pinning occurs within the relationship. A good adult dog mentor uses just enough pressure with their teeth to impart a lasting lesson, even if a bit of blood is shed. In these instances, it's not really a 'fight' but a swift boundary-setting interaction that starts and ends in a flash.

Considering how effectively dogs correct each other, why don't we, as humans, follow their lead? Let's simplify things—make them black and white, right or wrong—and avoid the gray areas.

The two most common complaints from puppy owners are jumping and biting, which must be addressed immediately.

No Jumping: Puppies often jump for attention. They're excited and seek your touch and praise. However, consider the behavior you reinforce if you bend over to pet, praise, or pick them up when they jump. When does this become unacceptable? When they weigh over 40 pounds? When they're wet or muddy? Is it fair to allow jumping sometimes but not always?

Instead, it's best to discourage uninvited invasions of human space 100% of the time. Jumping on their humans can lead to dominance and ownership behaviors in adult dogs. Teach and enforce boundaries from the start when shaping a puppy's behavior. Imagine a dog entering your personal space as equivalent to someone entering your home without an invitation. Maintain the rule: "Don't enter my space unless I invite you."

Four on the Floor: Enforcing this rule is straightforward. When a puppy invades your space, elevate your internal energy and step toward the pup, envisioning that you have a hula hoop boundary, and they must step back and respect your personal space. Be calm, firm, and straightforward. Avoid excessive excitement, high energy, or bending over, as it can be misinterpreted as play. Your goal is to make them move away and respect your space.

While redirecting can be successful in some cases, turning your back or using toys often becomes confusing and may egg them on to jump more; a quick, firm, and concise message works best: DO NOT JUMP ON ME! You could mark this correction with a name such as "OFF"; however, realize that you are first shaping behavior with the physical approach and then naming it. Simply saying OFF without using a form of correction often will not stop the behavior.

Remember, this uncomfortable stimulus only involves you assertively stepping towards and into them for their unwanted jumps and invasion of your space. The biggest reason that puppies jump is that the humans initiate it! Show me a human dog lover who is not happy and emotional when they see a puppy.

Let's separate the 'Dog Lover' from the knowledgeable 'Dog Trainer'. Training a dog incorporates behavior shaping and molding. When I see a new puppy, I initially ignore them so that they realize their status on this earth is NOT so unique that they are always celebrated or the center of attention. I must confess that I, too, want to run up to all puppies, squish, and snuggle with them, but as a trainer, I wholeheartedly know the consequences that my human behaviors can cause.

When the pup reads my body language of initial ignoring, they start to think. I base my interactions on the pup's state of mind. If they seem fearful or intimidated, I do not further put them at center stage to greet them. Instead, I ignore them and allow them to approach me. For the boisterous pups who want to jump, I first initiate by protecting my space and stepping toward them for their uninvited invasions. After setting my boundaries, I typically kneel down to their level and gently touch them with calmness. If they cannot handle me being down on their level and they keep jumping and invading my space, then I do not reward them with attention. I stand up and step towards them for any attempted jumps.

When interacting with a puppy, how can my touch, massage, and interaction relax them, make them bat their eyes, yawn, and feel at ease? This recipe has enabled me to teach all of my pups to melt into my touch and be trusting, kind, calm, and composed. I will detail this in my Point of Contact and The.Quiet.Kue™ section.

For younger children, who may be smaller and seen as playmates, teach them to play a game of "statue." Pups chase, jump on, and target children as they shriek excitedly and often run away from puppies. Instead, have them stand still, arms crossed, hands tucked on their sides, and look up at the sky, ignoring the pup. Instead of being a 'prey' for the pup, this statue game often deters a pup as the child is no longer fun.

If the pup persists, step in as the leader to stop the behavior by using a leash on the pup to control their actions around a child. Let's not let children become fearful or intimidated by boisterous puppies with needle teeth! We MUST act as the support crew for the child's space and help the pup learn that it is not okay to bully, jump on, or nip at children as they are fun and easy targets.

No Biting: Mouth contact from a puppy is considered biting. Play biting can escalate into more significant issues. Puppies initially learn bite inhibition through feedback from their littermates or Mom. Littermate play is rough, and they yank hard on each other. When the receiving puppy has had enough, they often shriek in pain, a clear message for the bully to back off and be lighter with your mouth.

Consider ALL puppy mouth-related actions on humans a bite and address them early. When a pup bites, gently but assertively grasp the top of their muzzle and wrap their lips into their teeth. The real lesson comes when you wrap their lips under and into their teeth, applying gentle pressure. This correction can be intense but effective and usually prevents chronic biting. The clear, immediate message becomes that when they put their teeth on you, they feel the pain themselves when your correction has them biting their lip.

If the pup seems overly intimidated, perhaps your correction was too harsh; however, the message was clear. Do not apologize or coddle for your correction if they overreact; consider it a lesson. Bold pups that come back at you even harder need a firmer and more uncomfortable lip pinch into their teeth. They need to realize that their bite is unwanted and causes pain.

Sometimes, you must make more extreme and explicit corrections to stop bad behavior. If your correction is not impressionable, it can simply become egging on or nagging, ultimately increasing your pup's tolerance. Dogs are incredibly accurate with their mouths, and biting is not a mistake. A dog that bites a human is not an accident. That dog either meant to bite, or he was never taught not to bite.

Allowing puppies to use their mouths on humans can lead them to see humans as littermates or playmates instead of leaders. While it's essential to befriend your pup, it's crucial that they also respect your leadership for their safety and well-being.

It's astonishing when clients proudly display scratches and scabs from their puppies, often dismissing it as regular play. In reality, allowing puppies to mouth and put teeth on humans can escalate into more severe issues in adolescence, revealing dominance and power dynamics. Puppy needle teeth may cause discomfort, but the potential for severe damage increases when these behaviors persist into adulthood.

Treating all nose bumps and mouthing as bites is essential. Enforcing this rule has not only prevented obnoxious behavior but also safeguarded me from potential harm during emergencies with my own dogs. A strict 'no biting' policy is non-negotiable in my book.

The message here should be unmistakable. Do not let your pup jump on you, invade your space, or let them mouth you. Early rehearsals of carelessness by humans lead pups to practice muscle memory responses, leading to ongoing behavioral issues. Many of my problem behavioral cases with adolescent or adult dogs involve dogs coddled, enabled, and overly nurtured by their humans. These dogs had a learned practice of control and dominance over humans through their invasion of space and successful bite response.

SECTION FIVE
THE MOLDED BALL OF CLAY

Two to Four Months

This book's central goal and purpose is to emphasize the critical importance of molding, shaping, teaching, and nurturing good behavior in puppies right from the start. By doing so, we aim to help dog owners prevent a wide range of adverse outcomes that can lead to problematic behavior in dogs, such as biting, dangerous tendencies, obnoxious habits, defiance/ lack of desire to train, resource guarding, aggression, excessive neurotic energy, fearfulness, and insecurity.

Your puppy is like a perfect ball of clay; it is your responsibility and opportunity to guide, shape, and lead them toward a successful adulthood. This book seeks to instill the idea that early training and positive guidance are essential to avoid the need for later rehabilitation work due to spoiled behavior often nurtured by excessive coddling.

Prioritize your pup's upbringing with clear rules, responsibilities, and curfews. Manners should take precedence over indulging, enabling, and merely showering them with love. Setting the foundation for a well-behaved and well-adjusted adult dog ensures a harmonious and fulfilling relationship between you and your furry companion.

Desensitize Your Pup: One of the crucial aspects of raising a well-behaved dog is desensitization, which involves extinguishing emotional responses to various stimuli, including negative and positive ones. It's not uncommon to hear statements like "My pup hates having his feet touched," "My pup is afraid of the vacuum," or "My pup is afraid of tall men in hats." Often, we base our pups' emotions on their initial reactions to stimuli, and we may inadvertently reinforce those emotions.

On the negative side, if a puppy runs away when, for example, a blender is turned on, avoiding using it or isolating the pup is not advisable. Avoidance reinforces their flight response. Instead, consider whether you, as a human, are afraid of that particular stimulus. If not, you must expose your pup to it repeatedly, gradually increasing the intensity, until they can accept it calmly.

Avoid enabling complete avoidance or overwhelming exposure. Find a balanced approach for each stressor, remain patient, consistent, and persistent with a clear purpose, and teach acceptance. Praise, high-value toys, or food/treats can be a great way to help shift initial fear responses.

Many years ago, I recall a puppy I had just gotten who seemed terrified of the vacuum when I tried to clean our sectioned-off puppy kitchen area. While it would have been convenient to say, "YES, now I cannot vacuum anymore!" That is neither feasible nor healthy for a dog to learn to fear everyday environmental situations. I left the vacuum out, unplugged and under supervision, and put pieces of the puppy kibble on the base of the vacuum. At first, the pup cautiously approached. Confidence was built, and the pup learned the vacuum was a puppy PEZ machine.

After a few repetitions, I turned the vacuum on, and the pup still approached the noisy device and readily took the food, which I first just put on the floor around the noisy vacuum. I then used the vacuum with my energy directed in opposite directions as I vacuumed away from the pup, yet I tossed some more high-value kibble or treats while I vacuumed. In no time, the puppy learned that the vacuum was something to look forward to, not fear.

Think of it this way: You might not enjoy visiting the dentist, but you're not allowed to bite them or react aggressively. You endure and show respect even though it's not your favorite experience.

Physical Desensitization: Physical desensitization involves touching, poking, prodding, and examining various parts of your pup's body, such as ears, mouth, eyes, feet, and belly. Even if your pup dislikes these procedures, your persistence and "won't take no" attitude will pay off when they need grooming, medical care, or examination in the future. The goal is to teach acceptance and tolerance, even when they may not like your actions. Any pup allowed to fight back or escape from such stressors learns intolerance and may resort to aggression when restraint is necessary.

When working on specific body areas, remain calm, patient, firm, and in control. Correct any biting, attacking, or lashing-out behavior immediately. This may involve lifting the pup by the scruff, giving a firm shake, or grabbing the muzzle to prevent biting. It might seem extreme, but teaching acceptance and tolerance early on can be invaluable during stressful adversities in your dog's life.

Practice frequent hands-on touch all over your pup's body, including sensitive areas like ears, feet, belly, genital areas, and mouth. Your vet will appreciate your thoroughness. Additionally, hold your pup off the ground, belly-up like a baby, to build trust and teach restraint. If they resist, don't put them down in a stressed state. Instead, gently restrain them until they relax, then release them slowly and calmly. As you put the puppy on the ground, remain in control even while you allow their feet to touch the ground, hold them still, and do not release them until they are calm, composed, and waiting on you.

Allowing a pup to squirm, cry, and demand to be put back down once you pick them up only reinforces their power and leadership. We focus on a conditioned response to being subdued by implementing our control while they are still very young. This control exercise aids in handling and restraint, benefiting later the adult dog's behavior when you need them to trust you, no matter the circumstance.

Desensitize to Noise: Desensitizing your pup to noise involves careful introductions. Live your life at home, using all your appliances, with the pup in their crate, which should be their haven. Give a high-value bone or toy so background noises in your home become familiar and non-threatening to them. Sudden, startling noises can be gradually introduced to desensitize them. Consider using a cadence of the noise or a gradual increase in intensity to help them adapt.

Implementing these desensitization techniques can help your pup become a well-adjusted and confident adult dog.

Socialization: Socialization is a vital part of your pup's upbringing, and how you introduce them to new situations can significantly impact their future perspective. It's alarming how often I receive assessment forms from new clients stating that another dog has attacked or harmed their pup. Puppies aged seven weeks to five months are particularly vulnerable and emotionally sensitive. Many have only interacted with their mother, who was likely nurturing and tolerant of their obnoxious behavior. When these pups attempt the same behavior with another older dog, it can quickly become an invasion of space or even an attempt to nurse or mount, leading to misunderstandings.

Unless I'm confident that the older dog is exceptionally kind and tolerant of puppies, I'm cautious around most big dogs. Introducing a young puppy to other dogs, whether in your household, with family, or with friends, should be closely monitored and supervised. The pup should be on a leash, and interactions with the older dog should be carefully observed. If the older dog appears dangerous or intolerant, it's best to separate them. Even if the older dog engages in play, keeping the pup on a leash with close supervision for the first few months can be a wise precaution.

Just as you wouldn't throw a budding football PEE WEE toddler into a big league NFL game, you shouldn't subject a young puppy to interactions with larger dogs without caution. It's essential to prioritize your pup's safety and well-being. Letting puppies play with others of similar age and size during their early months can provide valuable lessons in socialization. However, always step in and correct or separate puppies if play turns into bullying. As pups reach five to six months, they typically become more socially responsible and can be introduced to older, larger dogs under supervision.

Regarding socializing with people, there are various thoughts and practices. My consistent rule is to consider how I want the adult dog to behave. Enabling excited or overwhelming greetings from humans can lead to submissive urination, jumping, excessive excitement, or anxiety in puppies. Instead, aim for calm and respectful greetings, which should be the ultimate goal. Whether it's your college-age son or frail grandmother, the difference between a puppy jumping on them can be a severe injury. Teaching your pup to greet all humans politely and calmly from the start is crucial.

Conditioning Healthy Human Greetings: When greeting a puppy, it's crucial to approach the interaction with purpose and training rather than overwhelming emotion. Racing towards a pup with excitement can be traumatizing, invasive, and frightening, leading to anxiety or submissive peeing. Humans often view high levels of excitement in dogs as happiness, but this can signify an unstable behavioral state.

Excitement is a high-arousal state associated with elevated heart rates, blood pressure, respiration, and poor impulse control. It's a form of stress.

So, how should you greet a puppy effectively? Start by acknowledging and greeting their humans first. Ignore the initial greeting with the pup. Only respond when the puppy is calm, still, and stable.

If a puppy cannot control their emotions and become calmly composed, there should be no greeting. Praising excited or aroused behavior only reinforces stress. Delay immediate greetings, allowing the pup to use its nose and approach you calmly. Correct by stepping into pups who attempt to jump or invade your space, establishing boundaries and personal space. Demonstrate leadership by setting clear rules: no jumping and no biting.

When the pup is calm and polite, gently, calmly, and respectfully touch, reward, shape, and praise those emotions and behaviors. Massage the pup with kind and rewarding hands to create a strong bond. Gentle touch and massage can help to initiate relaxation and calmness.

Unfortunately, when raising puppies for clients, I often limit their interactions with most people. **People claim, "It's fine, he can jump; I LOVE dogs!"** They typically get the pup excited and jumping. I'd rather have my pup interact only with the right people while I mold and shape their social skills. If someone can help the pup be successful, I will allow them the opportunity to interact. Many people prioritize their love for the pup over respecting its needs, which can be selfish.

Here's a clever approach to use. A little white lie can work wonders when redirecting attention from a mischievous pup. Explain that you're training the pup for specific service situations and need help teaching calm greetings shifts the focus. It transforms the request from 'Don't let my pup jump on you' to 'Can you assist in teaching my pup that calm behavior earns attention?' It's a subtle shift that often leads to more cooperative interactions.

Effective Socialization: Socializing your puppy with various people, places, situations, and environments is essential. Exposure to different experiences helps them become well-rounded. Expose them to noises, stressors, unusual animals, various surfaces, car rides, and travel. The more they successfully experience, the more confident and adaptable they become. It's essential to create a pup that has been exposed to a wide range of situations and can handle adversity and uncertainty with comfort. Ensure that they associate their crate with safety and navigate stressful situations comfortably. Strive for a balanced approach, neither overwhelming them with stress nor coddling them excessively. Finding this balance helps your pup become emotionally stable, confident, and happy.

Interactive Play with Puppies: One of the most significant mistakes people make with their puppies is engaging in rough, antagonistic play. It's natural to enjoy games like chase, tug of war, roughhousing, and wrestling with puppies. The puppies, in turn, revel in the exuberance of these interactions. However, this can send mixed messages to the pup. Are you a litter mate and chew toy or the leader? When does the biting become too much? What if your playful chase turns into the puppy running away from you? These are the potential outcomes of rough play with puppies.

While these interactions may be enjoyable for you and the pup, they might not set the proper foundation for future training. Remember, you shape and nurture the pup based on how you treat them. You get the pup you deserve. Calm, gentle, and composed interactions create a pup that focuses well and respects human space, touch, and interaction. On the other hand, excitable, rough play can leave the pup stuck in a state of high energy and excitement around humans, ultimately a form of stress and anxiety. This can lead to an anxious and unstable dog that struggles with focus, composure, and learning.

My suggested approach to interaction with puppies is 'fun'ctional play. Consider games like throwing a toy with established rules, such as sitting before the throw and returning the object to you. These retrieving games provide physical exercise while molding control and reinforcing your leadership. The chase is the fun part, and the return of the toy to you signifies respect, communication, and adherence to rules.

The reward is another throw! Interactive games with rules set boundaries and release energy in a controlled and thoughtful manner, preparing the puppy for future obedience training. Teaching a pup to return a toy willingly helps deter future resource-guarding behaviors. If the pup won't readily release the toy, you can use flanking by grabbing its flank skin and lifting or pinching it, causing it to drop the object.

While flanking can be effective, it's not a one-size-fits-all solution when a puppy grips onto something. Attempting to pull can trigger defensiveness and a tighter grip. Alternatively, gently picking up the puppy and patiently waiting for it to drop the object avoids power struggles. This method is advantageous in delicate situations, like introducing puppies to game birds, where flank discomfort is a concern. Another option is using a leash to redirect their attention, often prompting them to drop the item voluntarily.

Avoid dominance games like tug of war, leading to power struggles. Tug can be a high-value reward for specific working dogs when used correctly, but for most pet owners, it's best to avoid it unless you are experienced in proper tug techniques. A tug game produces a high arousal state, and if you let go of the toy, the message to the pup is that he won, he is dominant, and now he can parade around with 'his' toy. He fought with you and won. Tug can also initiate growling, aggression, and fierce head-shaking responses, which are unsuitable lessons to practice with your puppy.

One of the best interactions with your pup encompasses long hikes where the pup can explore and follow you. If it's a safe area, allow the pup to be off-leash to follow you. In the first weeks of bonding, most pups readily follow their owners because they want to be a part of the pack and lack the confidence to venture off. However, they may become bolder as they grow, so using a long, tangle-proof line is a good option. These walks help burn energy, expose the pup to the outdoors, and provide excellent bonding opportunities with your furry companion.

Basic Obedience Skills for Puppies: While the primary focus during a puppy's first two months at home, from 7 weeks to 16 weeks, should be on crate training, patience, house training, manners, socialization, and desensitization, it's also an excellent time to introduce basic obedience skills. This early obedience training involves using a 15-foot cotton leash, maintaining a sense of humor, and having plenty of patience. There are four fundamental tasks we aim to teach: recall (Here/come), going to a destination (go to a place), being still (stop), and walking with you (heel).

The 15-foot cotton leash (see section on puppy shopping list in Section Two) serves as a means to guide the puppy through these actions. You can also use food or treats as a tool to help shape this behavior. Please think of the food as a lure to guide the pup into the desired actions rather than repeatedly using verbal commands in the hope that they'll understand. Instead, guide with the leash and lure with the food, and then name the action while they are performing it.

Remember, say the command once. Here are some examples:

- Lure the pup into the crate using a kibble of their food or a small high-value treat. Guide with the leash. As they enter the crate, name the action "Kennel."
- Use a kibble of food in front of their nose and lift it upward as you gently pinch their butt just above the base of their tails. As their butt goes down (moves away from pressure) and their head comes up, overlay the "Sit" command.
- Use the lure next to your side as they walk on your right or left. Guide with the leash and name it "Heel."
- From the kennel, guide them with the leash and lure them to you, saying "Here/come," and then finish with a "Sit."

These early actions, especially when the pup is hungry before meals, help shape the movements of going, being still, coming when called, and walking with you.

Maintain a calm and balanced demeanor during these training sessions. Avoid excessive use of words. Remember, we are trying to name the actions with the guidance of the leash. We cannot expect the pup to understand commands in a language they don't yet comprehend. Avoid repeating commands. You may only have one chance to recall here when they are running towards danger. Name the action clearly, as we will transition to saying the command and using the leash to enforce it. For now, with very young pups, we are teaching these essential skills in short durations.

While praising the pup for completing actions is excellent, keep your praise calm and soothing. We hope that being still becomes their default behavior, so overly excited praise can counteract the command/action you just taught. *Praise should be as powerful as correction, so use it wisely to reward the pup when they do something right. Avoid overexcitement that could undo your training efforts.*

Food, Toys, Bones, and Treats: The emphasis on positive reinforcement and redirection for unwanted behaviors has become prevalent in dog training. However, redirecting with toys or offering treats to curb undesirable actions doesn't align with a natural canine dynamic.

Consider a scenario where a puppy incessantly jumps on another dog. Would the recipient dog, like Spike, fetch a bone to appease the puppy? This approach can inadvertently empower the puppy and lead to possessive behaviors.

I advocate for a controlled approach to high-value items like toys and bones, encouraging their enjoyment within the safety of a crate. Additionally, free feeding by granting dogs 24/7 access to food may contribute to issues like resource guarding and aggression. While food is a potent tool for behavior shaping, it can also become a source of intense possession and protection for dogs.

How to Calm Your Puppy: A common question is, "How can I calm my pup?" A puppy can't simply have an off switch to calm down if they've been provoked into excitement. Even if you haven't intentionally stimulated them, puppies have a lot of energy, and they're frequently overstimulated and deprived of sufficient quiet time and sleep. By balancing crate time for deep sleep, calm interactions, exercise, and training moments, you can create a recipe for a happy, well-balanced pup.

Corrections vs. Molding and Shaping Habits and Obedience: Our primary goal during our first four months is molding and shaping our puppies, building good citizens, and preparing them for elementary school-level obedience. It's important to realize that you can only expect a puppy to understand or follow the rules with proper guidance. It's unfair to say, "My pup never listens" or "My puppy is so stubborn" when they haven't been educated yet.

So, what exactly is a correction for a puppy? A correction is meant to stop an undesired action at the moment. It provides immediate feedback for unwanted behaviors like jumping, barking, getting into the trash, biting, or picking up dangerous objects. Corrections should consistently identify the action, be applied every time the behavior occurs, and make an impression that deters the pup from attempting the behavior again. Correcting a pup with anger, frustration, or emotional intensity only makes them afraid of you.

Instead, isolate the specific action and apply a quick and uncomfortable consequence. It could be surprising, like a spray of water in the face, a quick scruff shake, or a quick, assertive clawed hand encounter to simulate a nip. Your emotions must remain calm and stable; you're not angry with them. You're guiding their behavior and providing the same feedback and quick physical correction as their Mom did.

On the other hand, we don't correct a pup for not being obedient. They are in the process of learning obedience commands (kennel, sit, here), so we should focus on teaching and molding these actions.

Your Behavior Around Your Puppy: Remember that your pup mirrors your emotions. If you greet them with excitement, your puppy will respond with excitement. While it's okay to allow some excitement at times, an excited dog can be unstable, making it difficult to focus and learn. Likewise, if you show anger, worry, or frustration, your pup will pick up on it and may become submissive or fearful.

Balancing your demeanor is essential. We want a puppy to be bold, eager, and happy to meet new people. So, brief new people to be calm and steady when they meet your pup. If they get overly excited, your pup learns this as the default behavior and may respond with jumping and excitement. This all too often can become the conditioned response if humans initiate with their excitement. Touch from you should encourage, nurture, and reward calmness, stability, composure, and relaxation. When you are calm, your pup will mirror that calmness.

Important Reminders: What NOT to do (NoNo's)

- Don't engage in chasing, roughhousing, wrestling, or physically challenging interactions with your pup.

This only puts you in a buddy or littermate role, not a Leadership role. The rougher you are, the more your pup will challenge you, growl, and bite you. What starts as play quickly snowballs into serious dominance behavior.

- Don't allow your pup to own your furniture or bed. You may invite them up to snuggle with you, but it is a privilege, not a right. The higher a pup is off the ground, the more they are in your space and feel equal to you. We must maintain Leadership. Invite pup into your space, and tell them to leave as well!

- Don't assume all dogs love puppies. Puppies are a menace to most adult dogs. Allowing your pup to jump in the face of or jump on other dogs is only setting them up to get attacked and hurt.

- Never free-feed any pup. You own the food; you put it down and take it away within 20 minutes if the pup is not interested. It is best to feed them in their crates and promptly remove the food if they do not eat. Re-offer at the next feeding time. This routine nurtures a robust eater, and you provide the food. A pup allowed to graze on food freely becomes a fussy eater, or worse yet, one who owns and guards their food. And the food goes stale. Hungry pups readily eat. Overfed or spoiled pups play games around food and become overindulged and fussy.

- Don't leave your pup unsupervised in your home. Either they are within your sight or safely in their crate. Out of sight usually means IN TROUBLE!

- Don't over-exercise or overstimulate your pup. Remember, their growing bodies and brains NEED 18 to 20 hours of solid sleep daily. The crate is your best friend to help them get the best uninterrupted rest!

- Don't give up on crate training! It is the MOST valuable training tool in your pup's existence. It keeps them safe, teaches them composure, and nurtures solid sleep.
- Don't ignore nail care. While your pup is young, small, and manageable, work diligently on teaching them to accept touching their feet and proper nail care.
- Don't let people meet and greet your puppy with excitement! This response only sets them up for failure. Excited humans create a highly aroused puppy who readily jumps, nips, or urinates from excitement or intimidation.
- Don't put your puppy down if they struggle in your arms. Teach them acceptance, tolerance, and manners. Subdue them until they relax, no matter how much time or effort it takes. Their puppy tantrums quickly morph into problematic, dominant, and demanding behavior if they can overpower you as little puppies. This behavior turns into unmanageable adult dogs who will not tolerate nail care, vet exams, or moments when they may need to be subdued to help them.
- Lastly, IF YOU DON'T WANT THE ADULT DOG TO DO IT, DON'T LET THE PUPPY DO IT! CUTENESS SHOULD NOT ENABLE BAD BEHAVIOR! UPHOLD LEADERSHIP, RULES, AND STRUCTURE; YOUR PUP WILL LOVE YOU FOR IT!

SECTION SIX
REPETITION AND CONSISTENCY

Four to Six Months

Okay, pup parent. You're doing great. Let's sit back and ask if there are any areas of concern you have now that you have a couple of months under your belt and you're seeing more of their personality traits and behaviors come through.

Identifying Areas of Concern or Red Flags

As your puppy progresses, it's essential to identify any areas of concern or red flags that may require attention. Here are some potential issues to watch for:

Refusal to Accept the Crate: If your puppy is still resisting the crate or showing signs of distress, it's crucial to revisit the crate training process. Properly crate-trained puppies view their crate as a source of comfort and security. Crate training is essential because puppies will most likely need to be confined at various times in their lives, such as during vet visits, boarding, grooming or travel. The crate is the best and most successful training tool to teach patience, manners, house training and to help keep your pup safe from environmental dangers. A pup that willingly accepts the crate is a pup that demonstrates composure and acceptance of rules, despite the fact that fun times can be going on outside of the crate. And lastly, they can get undisturbed sleep!

Messing in the Crate or House: If your puppy continues to urinate or defecate in the crate or around the house, it's important to reassess their house training. In some cases, repeated urination, especially if it's accompanied by frequent, small trickles, could indicate a urinary tract infection. Loose stools may also be a sign of an intestinal parasite, which is common in puppies. Consult your vet if these issues persist. If both of those tests prove no medical problems, then your puppy may just have some sloppy tendencies (often learned at birth and during the first weeks of their lives) and it just may take your pup longer to master the house breaking routine. Stay diligent!

Overreactive, Skittish, or Nervous Behavior: Some puppies may exhibit over reactive, skittish, or severely nervous behavior. While proper training can address many behavioral issues, some extreme cases may have a genetic basis. Skittish or fearful dogs often try to escape from stressors, and if they can't, they may resort to aggression. It's important to avoid coddling and rewarding this behavior, which can perpetuate the problem. Redirecting a worried dog toward constructive activities that engage their brains can be helpful. Truly training a dog with this type of behavior is extremely beneficial as obedience builds confidence and helps a dog overcome fear. For instance a dog terrified of stairs simply is unable to process how to use their bodies to navigate the obstacle. Using definitive obstacles overcomes an inability to problem solve through teaching them how to successfully manage adversity.

It's disheartening to see how often dogs are labeled with fears based on single negative experiences. A car ride resulting in motion sickness or an accidental fall into water can lead to long-lasting anxieties. Rather than accepting these as permanent limitations, I believe in the power of patience, persistence, and repeated confidence-building exercises.

By gradually exposing dogs to various environments and experiences, patiently helping them overcome fears, we can foster stable and self-assured companions. This approach opens up a world of possibilities, allowing dogs to embrace travel, water, and diverse interactions with confidence and joy.

Composed Human Greetings: If your puppy continues to jump or act hyper around humans by four to five months of age, it's a sign that they've learned this behavior based on how humans have been interacting with them. Training and engaging a pup in an aroused state can be challenging, so maintaining composure and calmness in human greetings is crucial.

Establishing a Bed and Teaching "Go to Bed/Be Still":
Introduce your puppy to the concept of a designated bed and
teach them to go to it and remain still while you watch TV or
work. This is part of destination training and involves teaching your pup the "Go" command. Use a specific identifiable
dog bed for this purpose, not just a mat. Using a leash, guide
your puppy to the designated bed and hold them accountable
for staying there while you're nearby and engaged in other
activities. It requires self-composure, thinking, and effort for
your pup to maintain this position. Repetition and guidance
will help your puppy master this command, which will be
valuable in future training.

Increased Socialization to New Environments: Now that
your puppy has received most of their required vaccines
between four and five months, you can introduce them to
even more new environments. Exposing your puppy to various settings helps them become accustomed to new sights,
smells, sounds, and surroundings. However, always manage
their interactions with new people, and coach those who meet
your pup to remain calm and help you reinforce composed
behavior. Be cautious about introducing your pup to other
dogs or potential hazards during this impressionable age.

Crate Training - A Lifelong Friend: The crate remains your
pup's best friend throughout their growth and development.
We can't stress enough the importance of using the crate
to teach self-composure and encourage rest and relaxation.
Many puppies and dogs tend to become overstimulated when
granted excessive freedom. With more space, they may feel

the need to protect and defend their domain, even with guard dog intensity, which can lead to stress and anxiety. So, the crate continues to be a valuable tool in promoting a calm and accepting environment.

Swimming Introduction: For those who welcomed their pups during the spring or summer months, introducing them to swimming can be a fantastic experience. Opt for warmer days and gentle water entries to make this introduction pleasant. Be cautious about abrupt entries, especially off docks or pool edges. Even in such cases, don't give up on water training. Learning to swim is a crucial life skill for your pup, providing exercise, enrichment, and training opportunities. Using a life jacket initially can ensure their safety. Most dogs truly enjoy the water, and by building their confidence with patience and persistence, you can open up a world of aquatic enjoyment for your furry friend.

Mental Engagement: While exercise and affection are vital, don't overlook activities that stimulate your pup's brain. Interactive games, such as retrieving and hide-and-seek, challenge your pup's problem-solving abilities and provide mental exhaustion, which is equally as important as physical exertion. Games that involve treats for stretching, bending, and balancing their bodies can also help satisfy your pup's mental needs while providing physical activities of lower arousal.

Leash Work for Stairs and Obstacles: Puppies often have limited awareness of their legs, especially the hind ones. You can help your pup learn to navigate stairs and various obstacles from around seven weeks old. This not only strengthens their core muscles and stabilizes their joints but also boosts their confidence and trust in your leadership. Employ a combination of treats and leash guidance during these exercises. Remember, it's crucial to prevent pups from jumping on or off high surfaces while their bones, muscles, ligaments, and tendons are still developing. Discover more through the QK Challenge Course!

At Quinebaug Kennels, our Quiet Kue training program incorporates a dynamic and interactive Challenge Course designed to challenge your pup's balance, confidence, momentum, trust, and physical skills. Our series of obstacles, including wobble boards, swinging bridges, pick-up truck beds, balance beams, poles, and hoops, engage dogs in problem-solving and encourage them to use their bodies for climbing, jumping, stepping on and off, and balancing. Beyond honing these skills, the course provides a foundation for light leash cues, laying the groundwork for specific obedience skills later on.

Encouraging Sit/Stand and Wait: Seize the opportunity to teach your pup the invaluable skills of sitting, standing, and waiting. Your pup will enter and exit the crate and the door to go outside countless times as they grow. Use these moments wisely to instill the importance of waiting patiently. An open door should not be an invitation to rush out; instead, teach your pup composure by having them wait politely until you release them. Picture your pup calmly sitting by the open front door as you sign for a package rather than darting outside into harm's way. If your pup attempts to bolt out of the crate when you open the door, simply close it in their face. They will quickly learn to respect an open door and patiently wait for your cue to proceed.

SECTION SEVEN
LEARNING TO LEARN

Point of Contact

POC, or Point of Contact, is defined as the area where a physical connection is made. When working with animals, POC is employed in various ways to communicate and teach them. Since animals do not have an innate natural understanding of the English verbal language, it is essential to instruct them in a manner they can comprehend.

One fundamental principle is the concept of pressure versus the release of pressure, or discomfort versus comfort. It's important to note that this concept does not necessarily involve applying force to the point of pain. The ultimate goal is to get our pup to listen to our commands and teach them in a language they understand. Think of leash pressure as a stimulus and the release of pressure as the reward.

In recent years, there has been a trend in society toward force-free or positive-only training methods, often viewing pressure-based training as undesirable. This shift parallels broader societal changes, including a decline in respect for authority figures and institutions. Interestingly, this societal shift has also been reflected in canine behavior, with an increase in aggression observed in dogs that have become defiant when asked to perform simple tasks.

Animals, it seems, inherently understand and respond to the concept of pressure and release even better than humans. Here are some examples: A dog lying in the sun experiences discomfort as the sun's heat intensifies (pressure/discomfort). The dog responds by moving to the shade, seeking relief and comfort (release of pressure). When a dog investigates a cat and encounters aggressive signals such as hissing and swatting (pressure), the dog backs away to avoid confrontation and seek comfort (release of pressure).

Teaching a young puppy to sit by gently lifting its collar to raise its head and placing two fingers (index and thumb in a squeezing action) on its rump to apply light pressure is a simple form of pressure and release training. In response, puppies instinctively move away from the pressure and seek the release of pressure, thereby learning the desired behavior.

In essence, pressure can be defined as any form of force or stimulus that creates mental or physical awareness, stress, or discomfort. The instant release of pressure leads to comfort, signifying the correct response.

The success of these methods can be attributed to the deep understanding and learning that comes from observing and interacting with dogs themselves. While there are various training approaches and resources available, the most valuable insights come directly from dogs and their natural behaviors. Here are some key reasons for the success of these methods:

Learning from the Source: The best coaches and mentors in dog training are the dogs themselves. Rather than relying solely on online courses, scientific databases, or behavioral experts, I have chosen to immerse myself in the world of dogs and observe their behavior firsthand. While I have had the privilege of studying with some of the best trainers in the industry, the dogs are my constant source of learning. Dog training is not a skill that you can learn solely from reading a book or taking an online course. When you can get your hands on hundreds and even thousands of dogs of all ages, breeds, temperaments and energy levels, those are the dogs that take you to school. You learn from your failures and build upon your successes. You assemble a tool box of methods that enable you to respond to nearly every action a dog can display. Each dog is a complete individual and various, minute tweaks here and there can be implemented to achieve even more successful communication. And often the tougher the dog, the more lessons you can learn. I learn from the dogs themselves every day.

Observing Body Language: I've spent years paying close attention to the subtle cues and body language displayed by dogs. This includes ear movements, facial expressions, interactions with other dogs, reactions to various stimuli, posture, movement patterns, and more. These non-verbal forms of communication among dogs convey a wealth of information.

Understanding Canine Communication: Dogs communicate with each other through various actions and behaviors. What may appear as a dog fight to humans is often a quick and decisive demonstration of dominant behavior, with one dog correcting another. True dog fights, where dogs are evenly matched in pack status, can be extremely dangerous and even deadly. These insights into canine social dynamics help build the training methods.

Importance of Early Socialization: I can't over emphasize the critical role of early socialization in teaching dogs proper social skills. Puppies interacting with each other and their mother provide valuable lessons in how dogs instinctively respond to stimulus, pressure, and the release of pressure. These early experiences shape a dog's understanding of social hierarchies and communication.

Respecting Canine Language: Shift away from human-centric, verbal communication and instead study, understand, and respect the language of dogs. Dogs have a rich and nuanced way of communicating with each other, which often goes unnoticed by humans. By paying attention to these signals and cues, humans can better connect with and train their dogs effectively.

Have you ever truly studied your dog's body language that shows your dog is acknowledging your communication and is in a thinking state of mind? When dogs are focused and open to learning, they will respond with subtle yet very definitive replies to your communication. Signs of their engagement with you include blinking, licking their lips, swallowing, and yawning. Their ear posture may be back and attentive or up and engaged with you. A dog is truly paying all of their attention to you if they have their ears and eyes on you.

They may also be looking away at their surroundings (still keeping track of you with hyper aware backwards ear poses).

If both their eyes and ears are focused on something else, then they are not engaged with you, they are focused on something else therefore most likely they are not in a thinking and responsive state of mind to your cues. They are distracted.

In summary, the success of these methods lies in my deep immersion in the world of dogs and my commitment to learning from dogs themselves. By observing and understanding canine behavior, body language, and communication, I have practiced effective training approaches that respect the natural instincts and behaviors of dogs.

Early forms of Point of Contact (POC) in dog training starts from the moment puppies are born and continue throughout their early development. These interactions with puppies are designed to help them adapt to human touch, develop resilience, and build coping mechanisms.

Here are some key aspects of early POC:

Handling from Birth: Responsible breeders handle newborn puppies from the moment they are born. This includes tasks such as examining the puppies, checking for any health issues like cleft palates, assisting with the umbilical cord, and gently rubbing the puppies to dry and stimulate them. Daily handling, which includes touching and gently stressing the puppies for various examinations, helps condition them to human touch and interaction.

Early Neurological Stimulation (ENS): Early Neurological Stimulation (ENS) is a crucial set of simple exercises designed to expose puppies to various stressors and stimuli during the critical period from days 3 through 16 of their lives.

Research studies, such as those conducted by Dr. Carmen Battaglia, have shown that ENS plays a pivotal role in the development of puppies, enhancing their resilience and coping mechanisms. The positive effects of ENS extend to a puppy's future behavior and adaptability. This is particularly significant for dog trainers and owners, as it helps prevent the development of fear triggers, ultimately contributing to a stable and more confident canine companion.

Socialization and Stress Exposure: During the first eight weeks of a puppy's life, they are exposed to various forms of stress, including socialization with human touch, being placed in different positions (such as upside down), undergoing medical procedures like worming and vaccinations, puppy baths, and experiencing nail trimming with a Dremel tool. Additionally, puppies are often handled and placed in a "stacked" show stance to evaluate their conformation. While these experiences involve stress, they also help condition puppies for future challenges and interactions. They learn early tolerance and acceptance to pressure and stimuli, and often their efforts to escape or evade are not successful because we can safely subdue and keep them under our control.

POC for Ongoing Training: As puppies reach eight weeks of age and beyond, POC continues to be an essential part of their training. This includes holding puppies in various positions, applying gentle touch to encourage stillness, using touch to guide them into sitting or standing positions, introducing them to crating, acclimating them to nail trimming with a Dremel tool, and teaching them to walk on a leash.

POC serves as the area where physical contact is made to elicit a desired response from the puppy, with the instant release of pressure serving as the reward for correct behavior.

The early touch and pressure applied to puppies prepare them for more advanced training tasks and help them develop the ability to handle and navigate various stressors. By learning how to respond to pressure and understanding how to turn it off through desired behavior, puppies gain valuable skills that will serve them throughout their lives. Early POC is a crucial foundation for a dog's ability to adapt, learn, and interact effectively with humans and their environment.

The Wonderlead

My training tool of choice is the Wonderlead. I learned all about this unique leash from my 15 plus years of training and mentoring with Rick Smith, son of Delmar Smith who invented the lead. I also had the opportunity to work with Delmar and learn training methods with his leash made most famous in the bird dog world.

Before we go further, I'd like to offer a brief history of the lead. It was developed by Rick's father, Delmar Smith, and got its original name (The Wonderlead) from another fine trainer, Ed Rader, who made the comment "You'll wonder how you ever got along without it." In the Huntsmith program The Silent Command System, it's called the Command Lead. No matter what you call it, it's an invaluable training tool.

The stiffness of the command lead is its major benefit. This stiff rope (also known as a piggin string used by cowhands for tying cattle by the feet) allows for a spring-like action as soon as your hand lets go, and because of the round rope release/ cessation of stimulation is immediate. When reward is quick, the dog learns more easily what is expected. We cannot over-emphasize the importance of a soft touch and light hands.

The Smith Family, renowned in the bird dog world as some of the most famous and legendary trainers of all time, developed the Silent Command System for Bird Dog Training. Recognizing the intelligence of dogs and drawing upon their instincts, this system is synonymous with the Smith family's expertise. Given that verbal words lack consistency in definition, tone, cadence, and more, they often only confuse dogs. This is why the Silent Command System is a powerful method of communication. This foundation is what inspired and shaped my own Quiet Kue system, acknowledging the effectiveness of silent cues and instinctual communication.

The Wonderlead is a preferred training tool that consists of a 6-foot leash made from rigid lariat rope. One end features a knot with a leather stopper, while the other end has a slip noose-style loop. This loop can be adjusted to fit over the crown of the dog's head, snugly securing it high on the neck just behind the skull. This positioning allows for light pressure control over the dog's head.

One of my favorite aspects of the Wonderlead is that it is uncomfortable on YOUR hands! So unlike soft leather, padded handles or soft rope leashes which simply encourage the human to hold on tight with excessive incessant pressure (this is the norm with almost all humans, watch how they grab a dog's leash and immediately hold tight!). Instead, this leash is rigid and somewhat hard, so as much as it cues the dog, it also cues the owner to use soft hands, with light communication ultimately with just two fingers used to maneuver and cue the dog.

One effective training drill with the Wonderlead is the Attention Drill, which focuses on teaching the dog to pay attention to the handler as the leader. Here's how the Attention Drill works:

- **Full Leash Length:** Give the dog the full 6 feet of leash while you hold the end with just one hand at the end leather stopper.
- **Direction Change:** This is best started in a quieter area lacking distractions, such as your backyard. Whenever the dog begins to pull or get distracted, execute a 180-degree turn in the opposite direction. This is done abruptly and accompanied by a light tug on the leash.
- **Surprise with Changes:** The goal is to surprise the dog with sudden direction changes, provide a quick and gentle tug on the leash, and then turn in a new direction. This tug represents the "pressure" applied to the leash.
- **Pressure and Release:** The tug and change in direction are the "pressure" points. The dog is encouraged to respond by following the handler, resulting in the "release" of pressure.
- **Repeat the Drill:** Continue to repeat this sequence of turn, tug, and go. You have mastered this drill when despite 6 feet of leash, any time you turn to go, you no longer have to tug because your dog has figured it out, by paying attention and moving with you! Begin to incorporate this drill on your walks. Any time your pup

starts to become distracted and forges ahead or tries to pull, simply change directions, turn, tug and go.

- **Cut through drill:** Once your dog really seems to be dialed in and paying attention, this next drill can teach them to be even more hyper aware of you and your personal space. Turn towards them and walk right through them. Meaning, when you face them, think of a line drawn from you right through them. Walk this line. Shuffle your feet a bit with an attitude of "Move out of my way!" The goal here is to have the dog move out of your personal space. Adding this communication helps the dog to keep out of your personal space, yet they move with you when you move away. It also sets the stage for later heeling drills when you turn towards your dog, they back out of your way.

- **Combine the Turn, Tug and Go Drill with the Cut Through Drill:** By systematically working these two drills, your dog will learn to keep their eyes on you, move with you, pay attention and move out of your space. They will first learn this within the 6-foot leash, then you can begin to make a loop at the end of the lead to make it a 5 foot, then a 4-foot leash. Before you know it, your dog will naturally place themselves at your side in a partnership, heeling position.

It's important to keep the hands light, as the goal is to reward the dog's efforts with a release of pressure. If the leash is hurting your hands, you are gripping and holding too tightly! The repetition of this drill teaches the dog to pay attention to the handler and avoid pulling on the leash. Over time, the dog learns to stay within a 6-foot radius of the handler, attentively following their movements, and eventually they partner up and walk politely at your side.

Key factors to remember in this training method include the tug as the enforcer of pressure and the release as the teaching moment. The handler guides the dog in seeking comfort by responding to leash pressure and following their movements. As a result, the handler becomes an influential and important figure in the dog's training, reinforcing a strong connection and attentiveness to their movement.

The.Quiet.Kue™

Developed from the bird dog training concept of the Smith family Silent Command System, The.Quiet.Kue™ is a similar form of training with the Wonderlead applied to all dog breeds and disciplines. We have successfully used the Wonderlead in our training programs at QK for over 15 years, and we teach every one of our clients how to use the lead. I am truly honored and proud to share this concept with pet owners particularly to spread the word and share the messaging that the Smith family has successfully taught within the bird dog community for over 75 years.

My dear friend and mentor Rick Smith was proud and supportive of my efforts to further share my own methodology and evolution of their system, and how I implemented our QK Challenge Course into our program to further teach, challenge and proof the training. Additionally, I experienced how successful their methods were within the bird dog training community, and I introduced the Wonderlead to all of my clients to include family pets and companion dogs. I saw how successful the leash and training system was, and it became my mission to equally share this style of training for all dogs (not just hunting), no matter the age, breed, or size.

NATURAL HORSEMANSHIP CONCEPTS

The evolution of incorporating Natural Horsemanship into my repertoire took my dog training skills to an entirely new level. It heightened my ability to read the subtle body language cues of dogs and respond with patience after they 'spoke' to me—through eye blinking, head drops, licking lips, swallowing, relaxation, and more.

In addition to my extensive studies with the Huntsmith system, I've drawn upon my deep-rooted love and practice of Natural Horse Training, honed over 30 years. Natural Horsemanship, with its roots in a kinder and gentler cowboy approach, shares principles that develop rapport with horses. Derived from observing free-roaming horses and rejecting old abusive training methods like breaking a horse, this approach aims to create a partnership rather than a system based on unnecessary force. The primary teaching aid is operant conditioning, reinforcing desired behaviors using a pressure and release system.

What excites me about applying this methodology to dog training is the firsthand experience of its effectiveness in horse training. Horses, being prey species, present a greater challenge, as they are more prone to a flight response. Unlike dogs, you can't simply drag and force a horse due to their massive size. Having learned to be savvy, light, polite, and successful in my horsemanship, partnership, training, and communication with a 1000+ pound flight animal, I realized the transferability of these methods to dogs. Through precise timing, reading the animal, and applying and releasing pressure to elicit a response, the addition of Natural Horsemanship concepts to my dog training became a game changer!

Top of Form

The.Quiet.Kue™ system is a unique form of communication and training methodology used with dogs. Unlike traditional training methods that heavily rely on English verbal commands with emotional voice inflections, The.Quiet.Kue™ system prioritizes a non-verbal approach based on light touch and Point of Contact (POC). The objective is to teach dogs specific movements and actions using gentle physical cues.

In The.Quiet.Kue™ system, dogs are trained to respond to subtle touches and cues instead of spoken language. These cues are communicated through physical contact, typically involving light touches or pressures applied at specific POCs on the dog's body. The system aims to convey commands and instructions without the need for extensive verbal communication. Effectively, we are now speaking their non-verbal language based on body language and the application of a stimulus to convey a desired outcome or response.

The core actions that The.Quiet.Kue™ system focuses on include:

- Walk with Me (Heel): Teaching the dog to walk calmly and closely by the handler's side without pulling on the leash. This is a join up or partnership.

- Be Still (Sit, Stand, Lie Down): Training the dog to assume a calm and composed posture, whether sitting, standing, or lying down.
- Go Away (Place): Guiding the dog to move to a designated location or position.
- Recall (Come Here): Teaching the dog to return promptly to the handler upon hearing the recall command.

The.Quiet.Kue™ system emphasizes calmness, repetition, and partnership. It aims to engage the dog in a focused, relaxed and tranquil stable state of mind, as opposed to anxiety, excitement, hyperactivity, antagonism or aggression. By maintaining a calm and quiet demeanor as a handler, the goal is to guide the dog to respond to The.Quiet.Kue™ cues.

Escape or bolting, freezing or fighting behaviors are all part of the RESISTANCE phase. These are normal reactions and they initially are discouraged through nurturing, teaching, and guidance, with the use of non-verbal cues and consequences. The system promotes a partnership between the handler and the dog, where communication primarily relies on these non-verbal light cues.

Once the dog has consistently responded to The.Quiet. Kue™ cues through repetition, respect, teaching, and guidance, specific verbal names (e.g., sit, place, here) may be assigned to each action. However, it's essential to remember that, even when using verbal commands, the dog's understanding of body language actions remains paramount. The.Quiet.Kue™ system places a strong emphasis on respecting the dog's perspective and focusing on non-verbal communication to foster a harmonious partnership between humans and dogs. The owner/trainer/handler learns to focus on and study the dog's body language just as much as the dog naturally studies our own body language.

In dog training, establishing and using Point of Contact (POC) with the leash is a fundamental aspect of communication and obedience. It helps create a strong partnership between the handler and the dog, enabling clear communication and desired behaviors. Here's a breakdown of how POC is utilized in various training tasks:

Leash POC "Heel" or Walk with Me (The Working Walk): The goal here is to have the dog walk politely and attentively by the handler's side, referred to as "heeling." The key is to establish this as the dog's comfort zone, rather than a rigid military-style position. A working walk should be a time of partnership, leadership, and bonding. The handler becomes the driver, and the dog follows, mimicking movements, stops, and turns. This level of engagement requires concentration, problem-solving thinking and engagement from the dog. This work feeds their brains and nourishes the need to work. The dogs become satiated by delving deep into their thinking minds.

POC Be Still: This aspect of training focuses on teaching the dog to sit or stand still while in the HEEL position. The leash neck POC is used to guide the dog into the desired sitting or standing posture. The Be Still focuses on teaching a dog to compose themselves with calmness while being greeted, touched, or handled.

POC Go to Place: This training teaches the dog to move away from the handler to a specific, identifiable spot, often referred to as "place" training. It's particularly useful for commands like "go to bed" at home or "go quest/hunt" in the field. The neck POC cues guide the dog to the designated location. This destination training is very identifiable to a dog and gives them a specific target with clear information.

POC Recall or Come to Me: The recall command, often referred to as "come to me" or simply "here," is crucial for safety and obedience. It involves using the neck POC to draw the dog toward the handler. This command is essential both in everyday situations and in the field. It can mean returning to the handler, coming close, or completing a retrieve task.

Summary of Leash POC: The leash POC serves as the foundation of a light-touch training system. It involves teaching the dog to respond to gentle pressures and cues applied to the leash, directing their actions. Once the dog masters the leash-guided behaviors, these can be transitioned to an e-collar as a replacement or overlay. The ultimate goal with teaching light leash POC is to transition to the same lightness with a remote electronic collar cue to provide communication and information off-leash.

The dog very quickly learns the POC (Point of Contact) and they respond with the lightest of touch cues. The unfortunate truth is that their humans are harder to train. Hand most people the end of a dog leash and the first thing that they do is take up all of the slack and hold tight.

This is equivalent to me coming and grabbing you by the shirt collar holding tight in an aggressive, persistent, or incessant manner to control you, rather than greet you with a hand shake and respect for your space. Better yet why don't I just meet you with a two handed choke hold and not let go, but expect you to relax and act normally!? Watch nearly all humans walk a dog and you will see leashes wrapped multiple times around their hands, all slack taken up, and consistent and unwarranted pressure.

Remember that dogs move away from pressure, so rude and unknowing human hands with overbearing tight leashes only cause the dog to want to get away (pull) even more. The poor dogs are darned if they do, darned if they don't because they NEVER enjoy the reward of the release of pressure. When this applies to dogs in no pull harnesses, face halter leads, prong or choke chains, these harsher devices only put even more pressure on dogs, causing them to be even more reactive or just numb all around because they can never win.

Consistency is key when it comes to training our furry friends. Repetition can be useful, but it's more about reinforcing the association between the command and the desired action rather than mindlessly repeating it. Teaching through cues and guidance is a thoughtful approach, and it makes sense—dogs are excellent at picking up on visual and physical cues.

It's like building a language between you and your pup, a language that includes not just the spoken word but also body language, leash cues, and the whole communication package. And the end goal is to have them respond promptly, especially in situations where their safety is at stake.

So, let's make sure each command is crystal clear, and once they've nailed it with the help of cues and guidance, the verbal command becomes a concise label for the action.

Weaning off Treats as Motivators: While treats can be effective motivators in dog training to initially shape behavior, the goal is to gradually reduce their dependence. This means transitioning from using treats for every desired behavior to rewarding the dog intermittently or replacing treats with other forms of reinforcement, such as praise, soft reassuring touch, or access to a favorite toy. This weaning process helps ensure that the dog's obedience and responsiveness are not solely dependent on treats but rather on the desire to please the handler as well as respect their Leadership in the relationship, and the established communication through POC.

Why Not Verbal Commands: Repetition is mastery of all skills. Each human has a unique voice tone, cadence, pitch, loudness, clarity, and enunciation. When THAT human is the one who teaches, the dogs learn THEIR voice. Think how confusing it is if another unknown voice starts to bellow commands at different pitches, rates, or inflections. However, a POC touch is universal, so anyone can instruct a dog consistently and eventually teach the dog THEIR unique language. If the dog is confused, the touch helps drive, reinforce, and enforce.

In summary, POC with the leash plays a crucial role in training a dog to respond to various commands and behaviors. It establishes a partnership and clear communication between the handler and the dog, enabling effective training and obedience. Additionally, weaning off treats as motivators helps maintain the dog's responsiveness and obedience in the absence of food rewards.

THE.QUIET.KUE™ CHALLENGE COURSE

The.Quiet.Kue™ (QK) Challenge Course is an innovative approach to dog training that incorporates obstacle and training equipment into the leash obedience program. This course was developed to add variety and challenges to the training routine, making it more engaging for both dogs and handlers.

The idea behind the QK Challenge Course is to provide dogs with a structured environment that includes various obstacles and equipment, such as wobble boards, swinging bridges, truck beds, ladders, sea saws, balance beams, a rocking boat atop a truck tire, and more. These obstacles serve multiple purposes in the training program:

Challenge and Variety: Basic leash training on flat ground can become monotonous for both the dog and handler. The addition of obstacles and challenges keeps training sessions interesting and mentally stimulating for both.

Building Confidence: Dogs are encouraged to navigate and interact with these obstacles, helping them build confidence in their physical abilities. This is particularly beneficial for dogs that may be timid or fearful. The obstacles present a very straight forward black and white challenge and each dog must learn how to use their body and leg coordination to effectively navigate the course all while being cued with the leash to encourage focus and willingness to try.

Enhancing Leash Skills: The obstacles intensify leash resistance and unwillingness to follow light leash Point of Contact (POC) cues. Simple tasks such as stepping up onto a platform when cued simply just blows most dog's minds! While these same dogs can easily scale countertops at home or jump on king sized beds, they fall apart when you ask them to try these obstacles on our terms. This resistance can reveal a dog's threshold level and areas where they may need additional training.

Teaching Problem Solving: Dogs are challenged to think and problem-solve as they navigate the obstacles. This mental engagement is an essential aspect of training.

Building Trust and Partnership: Handlers guide dogs through the challenges using light, directive POC cues with leadership. This builds trust and strengthens the partnership between the dog and handler.

Promoting a "Try" Attitude: Instead of accepting a dog's resistance, the goal is to use cues to create a "try" attitude. Correcting any attempts to resist or fight helps encourage dogs to make an effort and it very emphatically helps to get rid of bailouts, meltdowns, and resistance behaviors that start with a bolt, then lead to bites on the leash, jumping at the handler and ultimately aggression. These reactions are all the result of fear, lack of trust, lack of confidence, or an overindulged dog that was coddled so much they never learned to face adversity because they were not required to complete simple tasks. The obstacles enable the handler to break down the reactions by setting clear boundaries. It is ok to fail, BUT you must try. You cannot flight, freeze, or fight. We will help you learn and succeed.

Nearly every dog that goes through this process exhibits a beautiful and remarkable change in their demeanor and body language. A dog that learns to problem solve, navigate even the most challenging obstacles and succeed portrays an amazing posture of self-satisfaction like they just earned a blue ribbon. You can truly see and feel their glowing self-approval. They are happy and they even prance!

Beautiful Behavioral Changes: Dogs' demeanor and body language often change significantly as they engage their brains and problem-solve. They become more confident, relaxed, and emotionally satisfied.

Overcoming Reactivity: The QK Challenge Course has been effective in reducing bite and bolt reactions in fearful dogs by helping them develop basic problem-solving skills.

Communication and Obedience: The obstacles serve as definitive objects to navigate, allowing for clear communication between the dog and handler. The skills learned on the course can be applied to obedience training in various settings.

Proofing Obedience Cues: Handlers can use the obstacles to practice obedience cues such as sending the dog to an obstacle, having them stay on the obstacle, or recalling them off the obstacle. This helps solidify the dog's response to commands.

Repetition and Muscle Memory: Dogs receive ample repetition and develop muscle memory in a structured and clear-cut manner through the course, making it easier to apply these skills in other situations.

In summary, The.Quiet.Kue™ Challenge Course is a valuable training tool that provides dogs with mental and physical challenges, builds confidence, strengthens the dog-handler partnership, and enhances obedience skills. Handlers can create their own course using readily available items to offer their dogs a stimulating and enriching training experience.

If you look around, our concrete and natural surroundings provide plenty of creative obstacles and challenges. From stone walls to park benches, tree stumps to slippery floors, and stairs to puddles, treat all of these factors as your opportunity to challenge your leash POC and teach your dog to navigate these obstacles with the lightest of cues!

SECTION EIGHT
TRANSITIONING TO OFF-LEASH TRAINING

Remote Training Collars

There is quite an array of remote electronic training collars out there, however I am most familiar and loyal to the once Tri-tronic collars, now owned by Garmin. The models that I recommend are the Sport Pro for family pets and the Pro 550 for larger dogs or field/sporting dogs. Garmin is synonymous with their electronics, and the most important factors in a remote e-collar are consistency, battery life, appropriate and variable stimulation levels and integrity of the product to emit enough range at longer distances upwards of ½ mile. Just like our smart phones, you get what you pay for. The typical range for a quality e-collar is from $250 and up. Anything less typically means that you will not have the range or the power when needed. While these collars may ultimately save your dog's life, it is crucial to have them reliable!

"The e-collar doesn't teach. It cues them to do what they were already doing on leash."

Rick Smith

Bird dog trainer, clinician, competitor, breeder, writer, American Brittany Club Hall of Fame inductee and current (2023) President of the Bird Dog Foundation, Inc.

While remote electronic training collars have faced a great deal of negativity and misinformation, they are invaluable tools when used correctly. Let's start by dispelling a common misconception: these collars do not shock dogs. Instead, they have two metal contact points that emit electronic pulses or continuous stimulation, ranging from extremely light to higher, uncomfortable levels. This stimulation is akin to a TENS unit, often used in human physical therapy, which generates a tingling sensation to reduce pain, relax muscles, and stimulate endorphin production. It is widely employed for conditions such as arthritis, in physical therapy, and in sports medicine.

In our Quiet Kue program, we introduce electronic collars after initial leash training. The foundation of POC (Point of Contact) cues, teaching dogs the four basic tasks of walking with us, staying still, going, and coming to us, typically takes about two weeks of consistent work to ensure a solid understanding of these cues.

Once a dog responds to these cues, we introduce the electronic collar in conjunction with the leash. The aim is to use the collar's lightest possible setting, which produces a barely noticeable tingle sensation, serving as a gentle reminder when activated. This sensation might prompt a subtle response like a flicker of the ear, the dog glancing in the collar's direction, a momentary pause in panting, or even a blink of the eyes.

The reaction is so faint that it is almost indiscernible. The success of your light leash communication has conditioned your dog to respond to gentleness. The ultimate goal is to use extremely light pressure to communicate and elicit a response.

As you continue using The.Quiet.Kue™ of the leash, simultaneously incorporate the lightest possible electronic collar stimulation with a momentary 'nick' of the electronic pulse. The dog's response is usually subtle, as the electronic collar merely offers a secondary cue to support your leash POC. This remote electronic collar conditioning process takes at least one to two weeks of consistent overlay, always in conjunction with the leash and with dozens upon dozens of daily repetitions.

The leash guides movement and the electronic collar reinforces the cue, teaching a new form of touch. With the four fundamental principles of walking with you, coming to you, staying still or stopping, and going to a designated place, you can perform numerous repetitions, particularly with obstacles, to integrate leash Quiet Cues with electronic collar nicks.

After consistently repeating leash POC cues and simultaneous electronic collar nicks, it's time to challenge your dog with situations that may tempt them to evade, escape, or give minimal effort. As the distractions increase, you may need to slightly increase the electronic collar intensity, promoting greater commitment, focus, effort, compulsion, and/or determination to complete the task.

Once again, the leash is there to guide, while the electronic collar serves to support the cue, simulating a 'leash tug' or with a different form of stimulus, motivating the dog to exert effort. The moment there is a change in behavior towards complying with your command or the leash guidance, the electronic collar stimulation ceases. The dog has the power to halt the sensation of the electronic collar nicks by performing the requested command.

An easy concept. You make the right
behavior easy and the wrong
behavior uncomfortable.

Here are some examples of when, how, and why to increase the electronic collar pressure: Imagine you are walking your dog, and you halt to issue a cue with the leash and electronic collar. However, instead of complying, the dog begins to sniff the ground and pull, or ignores your efforts.

As you cue and guide with the leash, you utilize a rhythmic sequence of electronic collar nicks (NICK pause one-one thousand NICK pause one-one thousand NICK). If, after 3 to 5 NICK electronic collar cues, the dog does not comply even with a light guidance with the leash, you gradually and steadily increase the electronic collar intensity until the dog changes its behavior and follows the leash cue. Always remember, you are in a position with the leash to guide the dog into action. You reinforce and assist them in turning off the bothersome and mildly uncomfortable NICK pressure by complying with the command.

Be SLOW and RHYTHMIC. Nick,
pause and wait for the response.

Reward efforts!

Remain very light with your leash cues! The leash guides them to the action, and the e-collar stimulation directs them with a stronger cue. The moment they comply with your leash lightness, the e-collar cues cease.

This pressure engagement is very similar to how we use cues with a horse. We often start first on the ground, teaching a horse to move away from pressure, but as we graduate to riding, it becomes another form of cueing. While in the saddle, you start with light seat pressure to move a horse sideways. That is the lightest cue; next comes adding some leg pressure, next more leg with some touch of a spur, and finally, if there is no attempt to move, you can engage a quick spur (MOVE!).

Pressure engagement is a systematic sequence. Next time you ask, you again start with just your seat pressure and only escalate for a lack of try. You quit instantly when the horse gives you a try response. Interestingly, you cannot overpower a horse, but you can use cues to communicate and ask.

Why not the same with dogs? We are stronger than our dogs, and we can certainly force them to do a task; however, this means we are doing the work. The more we use force to make them do something, the more they are no longer responsible for trying; instead, they are being physically forced.

Let's use more patience, teaching, and lighter cues of annoyance/mild discomfort. When the dog chooses to find a solution and shows even a brief change in behavior, the pressure stops.

The more animals understand how to turn off the pressure to find the answer, the more willingly they comply, and we are not subduing them with force.

Precise timing is crucial to solidifying your dog's obedience and encouraging increased effort and focus. Reward any early efforts by ceasing the leash or electronic collar cue the moment they attempt. Conversely, communicate escape attempts with instant feedback, causing enough mild discomfort at the moment to change the behavior. Most dogs initially react to pressure with a flight, freeze, or fight response.

When they attempt these actions, promptly correct them with a leash jerk for trying to escape or evade, then resume guiding with the leash and cueing with the electronic collar. It's remarkable how swiftly a dog learns to cease evading and exert more effort to complete the task when they realize their escape or fight response will be met with correction. For instance, if you ask a dog to climb into a new obstacle that may appear daunting, they might initially refuse by turning their head away, displaying escape denial.

When dogs learn to look away from an object, they are essentially expressing their unwillingness to try. They may be fearful, perplexed, or simply unwilling to make an attempt. While we recognize that it can be challenging or frightening, not trying is not an option. Training dogs to confront challenges makes them significantly more confident, courageous, and adept at problem-solving.

Dogs are intelligent creatures who must learn to confront adversity and solve problems, not evade them. The act of escaping or bailing out can easily be nurtured to the point where a dog cannot climb stairs, enter a car, walk on shiny floors, step onto a vet's table, and so forth. They are denied the opportunity to learn and attempt. Instead, they are coddled and enabled to the extent that they become insecure, fearful, and incapable of success.

Promptly respond with a leash correction when a dog opts for the escape, making their action uncomfortable. It is astonishing how often they will then attempt the task you requested. The simple rule here is to make the wrong response difficult or challenging and the right choice easy.

Dogs are brilliant at picking up on non-verbal cues, and it's often the most effective way to communicate with them. It's like developing a silent dance between you and your pup. The leash becomes a subtle guide, your body language a nuanced conversation.

Quietly teaching through actions and cues makes the training more intuitive for the dog and encourages the trainer to be more observant and responsive. It's a two-way street of understanding.

Navigating a dog's reactions and responding appropriately is a skill that aligns seamlessly with effective training. Once this foundational communication is established, the logical progression is to assign a name to the cue. It's akin to adding words to a language they already comprehend.

Through consistent repetition, your dog develops muscle memory and conditioned responses to essential commands:

go, stop, come, and sit. As you introduce verbal cues, your dog can exert effort in compliance.

If your dog doesn't respond to verbal commands, initiate e-collar nicks in a rhythmic sequence until effort is observed. Increase intensity if necessary. If compliance remains elusive, guide with the leash. Yet, discern whether your dog is genuinely confused, stuck, or obstinate—reading your dog is an essential skill developed through training, coaching, and diligence.

Always prioritize helping your dog, but if you sense distraction or obstinance to a specific command, systematically escalate the e-collar cues to a level they find uncomfortable. This refocusing makes ignoring leash guidance less appealing. Ensure the right action is easy and comfortable, while the wrong one is associated with mild discomfort. The ultimate aim is to transition smoothly to using only verbal commands.

Next, initiate e-collar nicks alongside assured leash guidance, gradually increasing the e-collar intensity until your dog shifts behavior and aligns with the leash guidance. Consistency and repetition will, as always, lead to your dog responding to verbal cues, requiring occasional e-collar reminders to enforce or intensify compliance. Prioritize remarkable effort over speed in your training approach.

In this phase, remember that your dog needs time to process and act upon your verbal commands. Approach the training slowly, patiently, and calmly, speaking clearly and authoritatively. Keep your voice softer than the pressure from the leash or e-collar, letting the tools be the 'jerks'—leash jerks or e-collar nicks. You are the composed leader utilizing tools to teach, guide, use assertiveness, and correct if required.

Ultimately, your verbal command is the lightest form of pressure. If your dog does not respond to your initial verbal command, systematically go through the next phase with leash guidance and e-collar reinforcement as your light cue. Anytime that you incessantly repeat verbal commands, you are conditioning your dog that it is ok to ignore the first commands. Think about how they MUST respond to your emergency HERE command if they are running out towards the road. Condition them in this training phase that when they do not respond to your verbal, they will receive a leash and e-collar stimulus as a reinforcing consequence.

As you progress, you'll find that, with a well-established foundation using quiet cues and leash guidance, the verbal command alone prompts action. This is the moment— you've transitioned from leash cues to e-collar cues. In the next phase, consider using a lightweight, long line for backup or practicing off-leash commands in a controlled environment.

If your dog fails to comply, even with e-collar cues, default to helping them. Use two or three increasing e-collar nicks, maintain the sequence, and guide with the leash to ensure success.

The entire process of teaching leash Point of Contact (POC) to e-collar POC to off-leash transition take a minimum of four weeks working daily to get the repetitions. After this period, continued practice and proofing are crucial. Proofing involves introducing higher distractions, like other dogs or people. In such situations, be prepared to increase leash or e-collar pressure to regain focus. Always return to the lightest cue your dog can feel—ultimately, it will be your unique verbal command.

Proofing also exposes dogs to potential escape routes, such as bolting back home or towards distractions that momentarily captivate them more than their desire to comply. This phase is a normal part of training, as dogs sometimes reach their limits or succumb to high distractions. These moments are valuable learning opportunities—address the escape attempt and reinforce the completion of the command.

While some instances may feel like you are setting your dog up for failure, these well-planned and well-timed moments are opportunities to enforce. They are also when dogs grasp that higher pressure levels mean more significant effort. If a dog resorts to fight, freeze, or flight under intensified e-collar or leash pressure, it indicates a lack of understanding in turning off the pressure. Their resistance could stem from fear, confusion, obstinance, or dominance. Regardless, the training goal is to navigate this resistance toward a state of compliance, communication, and partnership with your dog.

Eliminating Trash Breaking Behaviors

The e-collar serves as a correction tool in specific situations, particularly in what is commonly known as "Trash Breaking." While >95% of our communication through the e-collar involves subtle cues for guidance, there are critical moments where a higher level is warranted to deter a dog from potentially dangerous actions.

Trash breaking, although an abrupt correction, is not aimed at causing lasting pain but rather making a significant impression. The e-collar's impact, even at its highest setting, is minor compared to the potential dangers averted—such as ingesting harmful substances or chasing into traffic.

Approaches to Trash Breaking

Setting Off-Limits Boundaries:
Establish an 'off-limits' boundary **WITHOUT** your presence for behaviors like counter surfing.

- Place high-value food at the counter's edge, observing from a hidden vantage point.
- Without verbal correction, let the dog approach. When they commit to jumping, apply a high-level continuous e-collar correction for 2 seconds.
- Though uncomfortable, this method imparts an immediate and decisive consequence, deterring the dog from the action.
- While it might be challenging to watch, this setup is a proactive measure to safeguard your dog's life from potential hazards on counters, such as medications and packaged food.

Applicability:
This method is versatile and can be applied to behaviors like carrying rocks, eating feces, accessing the litter box, raiding the garbage, or jumping onto windows.

The ultimate goal of this approach is to discourage the dog from engaging in these actions, prioritizing their safety and well-being.

Trash Breaking Method Two

Marking the behavior **WITHIN** your presence:
The second approach to trash breaking involves marking the behavior before issuing a correction—a valuable training

method that employs a cue (verbal or e-collar tone) to signal a warning before the corrective action. This method informs the dog its current action is unacceptable, and consequences will follow, and they MUST follow!

Example: Dealing with a chronic poop eater.

- Identifiable Marker: In the moment of the action, use a consistent and authoritative marker. For instance, say "LEAVE IT" with emphasis.
- Immediate Correction: Immediately following the verbal marker, issue an appropriate correction during the training phase. The goal is to empower the command "LEAVE IT" with a tangible consequence.
- This command extends beyond curbing undesirable behaviors like eating feces—it becomes a powerful tool applicable to various situations, from interacting with human guests to avoiding places they shouldn't explore (e.g., litter box, coffee table with food).

Building Power:

Providing an appropriate correction after issuing the command strengthens its impact. The ultimate aim is for the dog to associate "LEAVE IT" with the anticipation of correction, even when you can't physically correct them.

The Invisible Fence System Comparison

This marking concept bears a resemblance to invisible fence systems. During the training phase, the boundary is marked with flags. Dogs are brought close to the boundary, and a correction follows a collar warning tone if they persist. During this training phase, the dogs are on a leash, and when they approach the flags and hear the tone, they are purposely pulled into the invisible fence and receive quite a high level of correction.

At this moment, the fence boundary trainer will pull the dog back inside the boundary so that they learn how to turn the pressure off to stay safely contained. This process is repeated along several boundary areas to teach the dog first with a visual flag, then with the warning tone, and then they must feel the pain when they venture into the fence. Fences are set to a higher level to inflict pain because the consequence must be a strong deterrent from high-value distractions such as running squirrels, other dogs, or anything that may highly entice them to chase. Feeling the discomfort of the boundary teaches them to avoid it, seeking comfort by stepping back into the safe yard area.

This is corrective training and while the intensity level is high, nothing can compare to the impact of being hit by a car because the dog did not respect the fence boundary.

Dogs not systematically taught this training might challenge the fence or fail to understand the boundaries, leading to avoidance or fear of the yard. Proper training ensures they respect the boundaries and freely enjoy the safe space.

Trash Breaking Across Behaviors: A Moment of Impact

Whether it's trash, digging, barking, or chasing a deer, there are moments when a swift and impactful correction is necessary. However, we avoid long, continuous, surprising, and uncomfortable corrections, which can trigger a flight response. Typically, if YOU are using the e-collar with the emotion of anger or frustration, you have failed. For example, when calling a dog to come, escalating immediately to a high e-collar level might cause them to bolt. Instead, start with light e-collar nicks, gradually increasing until compliance is achieved, always reverting to the lightest level afterward, which is the verbal recall command.

A crucial note: never employ a high-level e-collar correction in cases of aggression toward humans or other dogs. High arousal states can intensify with such corrections, and they are not suitable for surprising corrections near people, potentially leading to reactive behavior.

Best Practices:

- Always teach first with leash cues.
- Introduce light e-collar stimulation/sensation to communicate as a language supporting leash cues.
- When cueing, begin with light e-collar momentary 'nicks'.
- Never apply a high-level correction close to a human or other animal, as sudden corrections can provoke reactive behavior.
- Corrections should first be taught on leash with an abrupt, quick leash jerk. This more intense Point of Contact touch prepares them for an e-collar correction. Subsequent e-collar corrections can later be applied off-leash.
- Corrections should aim to stop an action of infraction, NOT provoke fleeing or aggression.

Remember, the e-collar can successfully be used to halt actions—whether it's an "Ouch," a pause, or a complete stop—it is unsuitable for aggressive situations, especially when a dog is highly agitated or aroused (red zone).

The E-Collar as a Valuable Tool

E-collars, when used in harmony with a leash program, are exceptional tools. They provide off-leash communication that enhances a dog's quality of life. The freedom to run, play, and explore off-leash becomes a safer joy when coupled with the assurance of enforcing recalls and maintaining control in potentially dangerous situations.

Best Practices:

Methodical Use: During the training phase, consistently use e-collars in conjunction with a leash program.

Continuous Wear: Keep the collar on throughout the day during the conditioning phase. Avoid only putting it on for training sessions, reactive behavior, or to correct a behavior.

Avoiding Collar-Wise Behavior: Regular use prevents dogs from associating the collar only with training sessions or being used to correct rather than low-level communicative cues, ensuring they listen consistently. Refrain from displaying the remote with a threatening attitude (it is not a TV remote control, so don't pick the remote up and point it at the dog like it has magic laser beams coming out of it! Be nonchalant). The BEST way to teach a dog to be collar-wise is to not have the collar on when you need it, so you put it on after the dog's infractions and try to correct or repeat it. This only teaches the dog to listen when the collar is on. Do NOT make this mistake!

Despite this coaching, I still cannot believe how many clients tell me, "All I have to do is pick up the remote and point it at them, and they listen." Or "Funny, he only listens with his e-collar on" " (Ok, then be more consistent and keep the e-collar on during his waking hours, off at night) Or "He acts pouty when I put the collar on; he hates that collar." These comments clearly show that the owner is NOT using the collar properly, consistently, or as light cues.

If you stop practicing the light cue communication, the dog forgets the language.

Building Respect: The goal is for the dog to respect you and your commands, viewing the collar as a safety measure akin to a seat belt or insurance policy.

Post-Training Use: Even after completing the training phase, continue using the collar for several months to ensure consistent response to verbal cues. Periodically practice e-collar cueing language to reinforce their application.

High Distraction Situations: The collar remains a valuable enforcement tool in high-distraction settings or situations demanding immediate recall (public parks, near roads).

Think of the e-collar as a tool that, when used thoughtfully, fosters a deeper bond and understanding between you and your canine companion, providing a safety net for their well-being and freedom.

Will I always need an e-collar? Most likely not. However, once again, why not view it as an insurance policy any time your dog is off-leash? There are so many potential dangers out there, and the e-collar gives you immediate communication and control, which could potentially save your dog's life.

CONCLUSION

Congratulations, and heartfelt thanks for joining me on this journey through the pages of this book. It has been an honor to share a lifetime of learning and passion for understanding, raising, and living harmoniously with dogs. My ultimate aim was to foster even better relationships between dogs and their cherished owners. If you've transcended from being a 'dog lover' to a 'respecter of dogs,' I consider my mission accomplished.

In today's society, dogs are often treated as objects of human selfishness rather than truly understood as animals with unique needs. A dog can fill your heart with love and touch your soul like no other being. Their loyalty is unmatched and deserving of profound respect. We must comprehend their needs and strive to meet those requirements rather than nurture anthropomorphic qualities that humans tend to project onto their canine companions.

Whether you embarked on this book deep into your journey as a dog owner or as you contemplated your first-ever canine companion, I hope my teachings and stories have provided you with insights, ideas, facts, and reflections on how to become an even better dog owner. Dog training, behavior, and husbandry are not acquired solely through online courses or reading books. To truly know dogs is to live with them, immersing yourself in the world of dogs of all ages, breeds, sizes, temperaments, and backgrounds. These beautiful creatures impart new lessons about themselves, others, and even yourself.

When you can achieve balance, wellness, and peace around dogs, you become a master of leadership and pack harmony. I feel truly blessed to live in a space of love and harmony with my dogs.

If you are interested in training your pup, please check out Mastering Canine Communication: The Power of The. Quiet.Kue™ where I discuss our particular training methods and resources in more detail.

Happy puppy rearing!

WHO IS JENNIFER BROOME?

Jennifer Broome's life revolves around her deep love for dogs and the great outdoors, making her a sought-after authority in the world of sporting dog training and obedience for companion dogs.

QK also known as Quinebaug Kennels traces its origins to 2001 when Jennifer Broome, a dedicated dog enthusiast with a wealth of experience, founded the company. Her journey in the world of dogs began at a young age, starting with dog walking and pet sitting services in her neighborhood. Jennifer quickly gained a reputation for her loving care and unwavering dedication to the furry companions she looked after.

Jennifer's love for animals and the outdoors led her to pursue a degree in Wildlife Biology and Management at the University of Rhode Island, which she successfully completed in 1995. During this time, she also delved into breeding and training her own Labrador Retrievers, which drew the attention of other dog owners seeking obedient and well-trained companions.

Recognizing her innate talent and passion for canine training, Jennifer began offering dog training services part time in addition to her full-time role as a Wildlife Biologist. As her skills became widely known, she opened a kennel in Southern Rhode Island, marking the beginning of her professional career in dog training and care. In 1997, she officially transitioned to full-time dog training and boarding services, steadily gaining recognition as a talented dog trainer and kennel owner.

As Jennifer's life centers on her profound passion for dogs and the vast outdoors, with proficiency extending to training dogs of all breeds in fundamental, advanced, and problem obedience, she distinctly focuses on honing the skills of hunting dogs.

In 2005, she entered the arena of AKC hunt tests and field trial retriever competitions, a venture that not only bolstered her reputation but also elevated her credentials in the field thus solidifying her status as a highly sought-after authority in the realm of sporting dog training and obedience.

Over the years, Jennifer has amassed a remarkable record of achievements in the world of dog training and competitions, with notable accomplishments in AKC retriever hunt tests and field trials. Jennifer has successfully competed in sporting dog competitions spanning across the USA, showcasing her dedication to the sport. Jennifer also dedicates her time to volunteering as a gunner in numerous retriever field trials, and she has had the privilege of attending multiple retriever field trial Nationals, where she contributed as a bird thrower or assisted the esteemed Canine Sporting Veterinarian, Dr. Jennell Appel.

In addition to her achievements with retrievers, Jennifer has experienced remarkable success with her German Shorthaired Pointers. Notably, her GSP Elsie achieved an AKC Show Champion title, showed at the esteemed Westminster Dog Show at Madison Square Garden and excelled in Junior, Senior, and Master pointing dog tests. Jennifer's commitment to the breed extended to the NAVHDA testing system, where, she achieved impressive results, including several Prize 1 maximum UT scores and securing the coveted title of "Versatile Champion" in her winning ways with yet again another maximum score at this National event!

Jennifer's dedication to pointing dogs persisted as she continued to focus on new goals. Significantly, she provided training to Doozy, who happens to be Elsie's offspring, achieving an AKC show conformation Championship and attaining a NAVHDA UT max score of 200 in the year 2022. Her current endeavors revolve around passing the torch to Gunnel and Gertie, Doozy's progeny, as they embark on the path of competing in AKC horseback field trials, with the goal of achieving Dual Championships. Both have already accomplished placement and points in the show ring and field toward our DC goal.

2023 brought an addition to her seasoned pack with the welcoming of a new member, an English Cocker Spaniel named "Betty Cocker"! Being actively engaged in pursuing spaniel field trials with Betty has added another exciting dimension to her canine adventures.

In her professional journey, Jennifer has cultivated robust connections, collaborated or studied with renowned figures in retriever training, including Mike Lardy, Pat Burns, Ray Voigt, Andy Attar, Kevin Cheff, Danny Farmer, Pat Nolan, Dave Rorem, and Dennis Voigt. Similarly, her expertise in training pointing dogs has been enriched under the guidance of esteemed experts such as Rick Smith, Delmar Smith, Ronnie Smith, George Hickox, and Brian Hayes.

Jennifer's commitment to continuous learning is evident in her engagement with various business coaches, entrepreneurs, and leaders. She strives not only to excel as a dog trainer but also to be a leader to her team at QK.

Her commitment to her craft led her to spend the past 16 winters training in North Florida and South Georgia, where she hones her skills each year among a community of talented trainers. Upon returning to New England each spring, Jennifer eagerly shares her newfound knowledge and techniques with her staff of fellow trainers and clients at Quinebaug Kennels.

Jennifer's dedication to the field of dog training extends beyond competitions. For 12 years, she served as a Pro Staff Dog Trainer for Cabela's, conducting clinics and dog demonstrations across the country, and continues to represent Garmin as a brand Ambassador.

Staying true to always expanding her horizons, Jennifer's diverse journey extends to the founding of the newly launched global company, Artistry Afield, specializing in Curated Sporting, Outdoor, Cultural Experiences & Gear.

She actively supports organizations such as Ducks Unlimited, Ruffed Grouse Society, Pheasants Forever, and Quail Forever, giving back to the community that has supported her throughout her journey. Notably, Jennifer's artwork has been featured with Ducks Unlimited, contributing to the conservation of wetlands through the sale of prints like "First Light" and "Block Island Bluebills."

Apart from her involvement with dogs, Jennifer is a passionate outdoors enthusiast demonstrating exceptional prowess in competitive sailing and endurance horse riding, boasting remarkable accomplishments in both fields. She finds joy in painting, crafting, and gardening. And, of course, following her true passion of living afield, engaging in fishing and watersports, honing her shooting skills, and indulging in trail rides with her Nokota Horse, "Tex" or participating in field trials with her Tennessee Walking Horse, "Merica."

Jennifer's active involvement in professional organizations include:

- PRTA (Professional Retriever Trainers Association)
- AKC Breeder of Merit for Labrador Retrievers and German Shorthaired Pointers
- Board Member of The Labrador Retriever Club (past)
- Member of the German Shorthaired Pointer Club of America
- Member of Women's Field Trial Club and Snowbird Field Trial Club
- Member of NAVDHA International and the Southern New England Chapter
- AKC Canine Good Citizen Evaluator
- Past Member of Colonial Field Trial Club and Yankee Waterfowlers
- Past Member of the University of Rhode Island Sailing Team, World Cup Le Lavandou France 2nd place

RESOURCES

Quinebaug Kennels (QK)

The world-class epicenter of canine care and wellness.

Based in beautiful Northeast Connecticut, QK's ongoing vision has been responsible for its prestigious reputation. This reputation was earned through its steadfast dedication to a quintessential, proprietary philosophy known as The.Quiet.Kue™.

With 50 acres hosting what they do and used to show the world how they do it, they focus daily on one simple, collective goal: the all-encompassing, long-lasting well-being of their guests.

Few are the places that strive to deliver thoughtful & responsible dog care and training in a manner that considers the continuing wellness of visiting dogs. From enacting a set of beliefs where soft touches and observations achieve a higher, unparalleled level of successful communication, to create the most peaceful of partnerships.

From complete sporting and companion training events and seminars to short- and long-term responsible boarding, proper care-centric grooming, and an array of complete rehabilitation services. From their prized (and highly-demanded) opportunity known as Vita Plena to their ability to care for senior dogs using nearly 30 years of experience in appropriate elderly dog care.

Today, many believe QK is one the few places left where they ensure a dog will genuinely live their life to the fullest...either while visiting or once they've arrived back home. https://www.qkdogs.com/

Artistry Afield

A sporting and conservation opportunity enhancing everyone's storybook life afield.

Founded by Jennifer Broome, a lifelong sportswoman, Artistry Afield encourages passionate, like-minded sporting enthusiasts to reach further and engage in sporting moments and opportunities afield unlike any other. As Jennifer puts it so well, "I wanted to offer our clients something uncommon and unique while also offering them the opportunity to learn something new that would move their passions forward."

Today, Artistry Afield is offering a line of self-designed field gear and accoutrements, exclusive sporting global travel destinations, and world-renowned, foundational puppy training, enabling sportsmen and sportswomen to ensure the best life afield next to their four-legged friend.

When it comes to their private product line, their teams' vast experience sourcing the finest raw materials and envisioning invaluable features in products uncommon in today's markets is just one reason why Artistry Afield is augmenting the finest moments lived outdoors. https://www.artistryafield.com/

DEVOTION SUPPLEMENTS

QK's All Natural and Proprietary Supplement Line Enabling Your Dogs Best Health & Well-Being

Envisioned and created at QK, the state-of-the-art epicenter of canine care and wellness in Northeast Connecticut, DEVOTION is a proprietary line of all-natural supplements designed to maximize dogs' overall nutrition.

As one may agree, a dog is what they eat, and it is clear those who show dull coats, weakened immune systems, allergies, or lick and eat dirt, rocks, or poop are not getting adequate nutrition. Being a proprietary line of fresh, quality-forward ingredients, each bag is made to order, enabling peace of mind to all those DEVOTED to their dogs.

Daily Support +: Daily Support + supports your dog's skin, coat, digestive system, and more with a daily vitamin/mineral boost and a healthy dose of natural Omega-3. It also contains custom-blend Probiotics and Prebiotics providing comprehensive joint support for active, working dogs, and older dogs with joint support needs.

Norwegian Dried Kelp: This underwater seaweed contains at least 25 vitamins, including vitamins A, B12, and folic acid, and aids in maintaining a shiny coat and healthy skin. Rich in vitamin D, calcium, iron, iodine, potassium, sulfur, and magnesium, kelp also contains sodium alginate, which is said to rid the body of heavy metals and radioactive elements.

Digestive Wellness: A unique blend of Prebiotics, Probiotics, and digestive Enzymes, it optimizes the absorption of nutritional supplements for overall improved health and well-being. It also stimulates and feeds beneficial intestinal bacteria.

The Delmar Smith Wonderlead: "You'll Wonder How You Lived Without It!"

The Quiet.Kue™ book is a comprehensive explanation of Wonderlead's history, background, and operation. It is the most effective training tool for creating a Point Of Contact to achieve lightness with the leash and provides the best Foundational Training for later e-collar conditioning. This special lariat-style tool is often imitated but never duplicated! Purchase online from our QK Store. https://www.qkdogs.com/shop

www.akc.org
Whether you're a breeder or a new dog owner, AKC is the trusted expert for all things dog. Learn about the breeds, dog sports and events, find breeders, and learn about the most up-to-date health and wellness for dogs.

www.akcchf.org
Canine Health Information Center, also known as CHIC, is a centralized canine health database jointly sponsored by the AKC Canine Health Foundation (CHF) and the Orthopedic Foundation for Animals (OFA). CHIC, working with participating parent club, provides a resource for breeders and owners of purebred dogs to research and maintain information on the health issues prevalent in specific breeds. Browse this site to see if the dog breed and breeder that you are interested in is currently enrolled in the CHIC program and what tests are required to obtain a CHIC number.

www.catooutdoors.com
Dog training platforms made in the United States. Safe, elevated, sturdy, portable and stackable. Once your dog understands "Place" on the Cato Platforms, you have a new gateway to good things! The Cato Platform can be used for almost any scenario – visitors at the door, control when being let in or out, feeding time, remote sits, recall, steadiness training, handling drills and upland field drills. With a little patience and creativity, the Cato Platforms will change the way you interact with your dog!

www.garmin.com
The leader in the industry for remote electronic collars for family pets and sporting dogs. From training and bark-reducing collars to GPS tracking systems, their comprehensive line of collars encompasses a vast array of sizes, styles and options.

http://www.healthypawspetinsurance.com/?affid=QK0
Top rated pet insurance. Available in all 50 states, Healthy Paws Pet Insurance has been rated #1 based on customer reviews for over seven years in a row. Covering accidents, illnesses, cancer, emergency care, genetic and hereditary conditions, breed-specific conditions, and alternative care. Please use our partnership link above.

www.huntsmith.com
Celebrating over 50 years of helping people train their field and bird dogs.

https://Kuranda.com?partner=16269
Dog beds that are orthopedic, chew proof and easy to clean. Kuranda's elevated dog beds provide a great relief for dogs' joints. The cot style design evenly distributes their weight so there are no pressure point like they would have on the ground. Kuranda's patented design secures the fabric side the frame making it totally inaccessible to dogs that chew. Guaranteed for one full year. Unlike pillow style beds that hold odor and hair, these beds can be hosed or wiped to clean. Accessory pads are machine washable. At Quinebaug Kennels, Kuranda Beds are our #1 choice for our kennel bedding AND they are a staple for our training programs providing an elevated, distinctive, identifiable platform to "Go Lie Down." Additionally, the bed serves as a destination for "PLACE" whether you use the bed indoors or outside on the patio to provide a definitive platform to stay on. Purchase online from our QK Store. https://www.qkdogs.com/kuranda

www.ofa.org

Orthopedic Foundation for Animals mission is to promote the health and welfare of companion animals through a reduction in the incidence of genetic diseases.

https://www.purina.com/

Nestlé Purina PetCare creates richer lives for pets and the people who love them. Founded in 1894, Purina has helped dogs and cats live longer, healthier lives by offering scientifically based nutritional innovations. Purina manufactures some of the world's most trusted and popular pet care products, including Purina ONE, Pro Plan, Fancy Feast and Tidy Cats. Our more than 10,000 U.S. associates take pride in our trusted pet food, treat and litter brands that feed 46 million dogs and 68 million cats every year. More than 500 Purina scientists, veterinarians, and pet care experts ensure our commitment to unsurpassed quality and nutrition.

Purina promotes responsible pet care through our scientific research, our products, and our support for pet-related organizations. Over the past five years, Purina has contributed more than $150 million towards organizations that bring, and keep, people and pets together, as well as those that help our communities and environment thrive.